DMU 0365723

KT-222-812

RY

mped

Serrasalmus elongatus. Photo by Leo G. Nico and Donald C. Taphorn.

The myths of the bloodthirsty piranha are perpetuated by the sale of dried, mounted piranhas whose lips have been cut away to bare their sharp teeth. The eyes are fake. Photo by Dr. Herbert R. Axelrod of Jerome M. Eisenberg of The Collector's Cabinet in New York City.

PIRANHAS
in the Aquarium

WOLFGANG SCHULTE

Serrasalmus nattereri. Photo by Hans-Joachim Richter.

T.F.H. PUBLICATIONS, INC.
1 T.F.H. Plaza • Third and Union Aves. • Neptune City, NJ 07753

This book was originally published in German by Albrecht Philler Verlag GmbH, 4950 Minden, West Germany. They own the German copyright.

© 1988 by TFH Publications, Inc., Neptune City, N.J. 07753 for the translation and the original illustrations. Those drawings which appeared in the original German work have been enhanced and colored by John Quinn.

DE MONTFORT UNIVERSITY LIBRARY

Date	19.6.97
Loc./Form	CAT
Class	639.34
Suffix	9876543215CH

1995 Edition

9 6789

Distributed in the UNITED STATES to the Pet Trade by T.F.H. Publications, Inc., One T.F.H. Plaza, Neptune City, NJ 07753; distributed in the UNITED STATES to the Bookstore and Library Trade by National Book Network, Inc. 4720 Boston Way, Lanham MD 20706; in CANADA to the Pet Trade by H & L Pet Supplies Inc., 27 Kingston Crescent, Kitchener, Ontario N2B 2T6; Rolf C. Hagen Ltd., 3225 Sartelon Street, Montreal 382 Quebec; in CANADA to the Book Trade by Vanwell Publishing Ltd., 1 Northrup Crescent, St. Catharines, Ontario L2M 6P5 ; in ENGLAND by T.F.H. Publications, PO Box 15, Waterlooville PO7 6BQ; in AUSTRALIA AND THE SOUTH PACIFIC by T.F.H. (Australia), Pty. Ltd., Box 149, Brookvale 2100 N.S.W., Australia; in NEW ZEALAND by Brooklands Aquarium Ltd. 5 McGiven Drive, New Plymouth, RD1 New Zealand; in Japan by T.F.H. Publications, Japan—Jiro Tsuda, 10-12-3 Ohjidai, Sakura, Chiba 285, Japan; in SOUTH AFRICA by Lopis (Pty) Ltd., P.O. Box 39127, Booysens, 2016, Johannesburg, South Africa. Published by T.F.H. Publications, Inc.

MANUFACTURED IN THE UNITED STATES OF AMERICA
BY T.F.H. PUBLICATIONS, INC.

CONTENTS

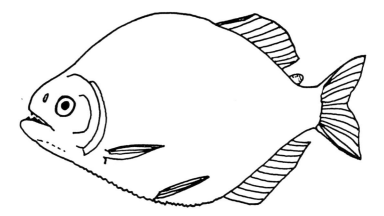

One of the earliest sketches of a piranha was created by
Alexander von Humboldt about 1800.

A Historical and Literary Critique

After the discovery of the South American continent by Columbus in 1498, it was not long before numerous conquistadores combed the New World, including the perilous tropical forests, in search of the imaginary golden land, El Dorado. Around 1533 a group of conquistadores set off from Peru for the Amazon with the Spanish general Pizarro. They were the first Europeans to catch sight of piranhas, described as "small, carnivorous, predatory fish that glisten bluish green." A monk described how, during an attack, Indians who had been hit by musket fire and by cannonballs fell from their canoes into the river and were thoroughly skeletonized in an instant by these predatory fish that were present in massive numbers.

On his journeys through Venezuela, Alexander von Humboldt also came into contact with the piranhas. On April 3, 1800, he wrote in his journal:

> *Near San Fernando on the Rio Apure. In the morning our Indians got out the rod and line and caught the fish known as* caribe *or* caribito *in these parts. The latter attacks human beings when they bathe and often tears sizable chunks of flesh out of them. Although the injuries are trivial to start with, one is hard put to get out of the water without sustaining the most serious wounds. If one pours a few drops of blood into the water, they come up by the thousands.*

This extract from the diary of the explorer Carl Ferdinand Appun sounds less dramatic, however:

> *March, 30, 1859. About to bathe, I had hardly submerged myself in the tepid water of the Inamara [river in Guyana] when I came back up again and retreated to the bank as fast as I could, having felt the bite of a piranha on my thigh where I had been bitten by a mosquito and scratched myself until I bled. These fish, among the worst pests found in the waters, make it impossible to bathe. Bathing is so refreshing and so necessary in this climate and quite excellent when one is traveling. Giving oneself a wash on the river bank is a poor substitute.*

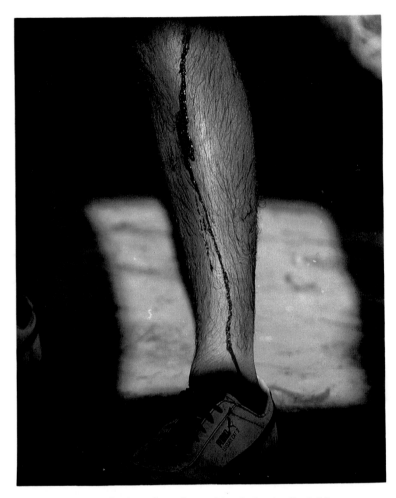

A piranha bite on the leg of a collector bleeds freely. Such bites are very rare and only occur during netting when the piranhas are in a frightened frenzy. Photo by G. Feo.

The aggressiveness of piranhas always has been, and continues to be, a popular theme with a wide range of authors who are forever coming up with new, still more drastic variations. One example, labored and exaggerated to excess, is the story of a sick cow having to be sacrificed to divert the piranhas from the herd each time the river is being crossed. The sheer number of rivers and the poverty of the herdsmen alone speak against actions of this kind.

Serrasalmus nattereri. This was a huge specimen, almost 12″ (30 cm) long. Collected and photographed by Dr. Herbert R. Axelrod.

The following excerpts from the book by Street will convince the reader that, when it comes to the subject of piranhas, even scientists get carried away and become emotional without recognizing they are making complete fools of themselves:

> *The shark and the barracuda are frightening creatures, but nothing that swims in the sea is as ragingly ferocious and dangerous to man as a small fish which inhabits the rivers of South America. This is the* **piranha.** *It rightly has the reputation of being a man-eater, despite the fact that it rarely exceeds 17.5 cm (7 inches) in length and 25 cm (10 inches) constitutes a record.*

A giant *pirambeba*, the local Indian name for this piranha. It was 20″ (51 cm) in total length and was brought back from the upper Rio Xingu, Brazil, by Dr. Herbert R. Axelrod, who had it mounted and keeps it on his wall!

Top: A Camaiura tribe boy fishing in the Rio Koluena (Rio Xingu).
Below: A Laualapiti boy who just shot a pacu (*Metynnis*) with his bow
and arrow. This is the Tuatuari River in the Xingu reservation.

Death caused by the shark or the barracuda tends to be quick and, as compared with death by the piranha, can virtually be described as merciful. Any human being and any animal having the misfortune to fall into the river in a spot infested with this blood-thirsty fish literally gets eaten alive. Hundreds of these fish suddenly appear from no-where and the victim's flesh is devoured in tens of thousands of small bites until nothing remains but the bare

A very large and hungry school of red-bellied piranhas, probably *Serrasalmus nattereri*, awaiting the arrival of stunned small fishes as they are flushed out of a culvert during a rainstorm. The Brazilian government built roads through the jungle. Small rivers were diverted under the roads through culverts, but as the area around the culvert outlets wore down from constant water flows, small lakes often resulted. These lakes became infested with constantly hungry piranhas. Under these circumstances, piranhas are extremely dangerous. Photo by Leo G. Nico.

skeleton. The horrible deed does not take long. In a more recent experiment the cadaver of a pig weighing 400 pounds was lowered into a river known to be teeming with piranhas. After ten minutes only the bones were left. Small though the piranha is, it possesses an unbelievably sharp set of teeth with which it can bite clean through a finger, bone and all, at one go. Normally the piranha is a calm

fish, but when a victim appears, it seems to go berserk, and what compels it is not hunger alone. Long after the fish have eaten their fill they continue with their furious attacks until not even the tiniest shred of flesh is left; the remains pile up on the bottom of the river until the current sweeps them away. No living creature escapes their attention, not even one of their own genus, and it is impossible to keep more than one of these fish in one and the same aquarium.

This style of writing makes one wonder what came over many a scientist who was otherwise so cool and rational when he dealt with the topic of piranhas.

Authors at times adopt the style of sensational journalism, not only in strictly scientific works but also in popular scientific works when they talk about piranhas. This is all the more serious since, generally speaking, the reader of such a publication is not in a position to appraise the factual content of what he is reading. Here in particular every author ought to be aware of the opinion-forming effect of repetition and strive all the harder to provide a scientifically accurate description. The sensationalistic tabloid press also likes to take up repeatedly the "horror story of the blood-thirstiest fish in the world." Thus the reading public is gradually being indoctrinated with the belief that this is what piranhas are really like.

So far, the most gruesome reporting of all was undoubtedly in the film *Piranhas—Only the Bones Remain,* which was shown in the cinemas in 1978/79. Slogans employed to advertise this movie included:

- *The killer fish are here!*
- *Sharks come singly, piranhas come in the thousands!*
- *Piranhas, fish that have tasted blood!*
- *Piranhas,...and they eat you alive!*
- *Piranhas, they tear, bore, bite, until only the bones remain!*
- *Human beings are smitten with terror as the killer fish advance!*

The entire film was filled with cheap horror effects (screaming, clouds of blood, teeth-baring plastic piranhas) and hair-raising falsehoods. At best, it can be described as a badly made science fiction monster-film. The new motto appears to be: ***"Dracula and Frankenstein are dead—long live the white shark, the killer bee, the deadly spider, and the piranha."*** The foregoing list could be extended indefinitely. New monsters rooted in reality are being produced all the time. Animals are presented as grotesque caricatures,

The famed explorer, fish photographer, and aquarium fish breeder, Hans-Joachim Richter of Leipzig, DDR, performs an experiment prompted by Dr. Axelrod. He went into piranha-infested waters in the Rio Abacaxis-Rio Madeira intersection and put a chunk of meat on a hook. In less than 5 seconds he had hooked a piranha. They only attacked the meat...not him! Photo by Dr. Herbert R. Axelrod.

Hans-Joachim Richter reels in the piranha. He continued fishing and in a matter of 30 minutes was able to catch 18 piranhas. At no time did any fish come close enough for him to see or feel it. Photo by Dr. Herbert R. Axelrod.

their modes of behavior exaggerated in the extreme. As for the thinking that lies behind all of this, the common criterion appears to be, *"The main thing is to make a big profit"*!

In reality, there are very few confirmed cases of human beings having been attacked by piranhas and dying as a result. The late Harald Schultz was an Ethnologist at the Museum of Ethnology in São Paulo and one of the greatest authorities on the Indians and wildlife of the Amazon region. During his 20-year stay in South America he came across only seven people who had been attacked by piranhas. With one exception, none of them had been seriously injured in these attacks. Prof. Dr. Herbert R. Axelrod, with 30 years of experience fishing in Brazil, says the same thing. Many inhabitants of regions that are at risk from piranhas swim and bathe in the rivers and lakes every day without concern. Generally, the natives are so intimately acquainted with nature that they know exactly where and when it is safe to bathe. Near Ciudad Bolivar, where the Orinoco narrows to 3 kilometers (1.8 mi.) in width, the few who can afford it actually go water-skiing.

In my opinion, many a piranha victim was, in fact, not attacked, let alone reduced to a skeleton by the fish, until he had already succumbed to a less spectacular death by drowning. Dr. Axelrod agrees with this theory.

In a small lake near Humaita (Rio Madeira), Brazil, Dr. Axelrod caught almost 200 piranhas in a drying-out lake. It took 2 hours. The fish were subsequently preserved and mounted and given away free as premiums to subscribers of *Tropical Fish Hobbyist* magazine. Photo by Dr. Herbert R. Axelrod.

When we traveled through vast regions of Venezuela in March
and April (i.e., towards the end of the dry season) many areas had
dried up; small rivers had changed into rills, and lagoons or larger
ponds had shrunken to muddy puddles. It is obvious that piranhas
now confined to a very small space and suffering the greatest shortage of food are extremely aggressive and stepping into such dangerous waters would not be advisable. On the other hand, in August,
during the rainy season when the rivers rise by 12 meters (40 feet)
in some areas (Rio Apure) and flooding transforms whole valleys
into flood plains, the piranha shoals that were so crowded before

Not all the piranhas Dr. Axelrod caught were preserved. He cooked some of them
in a frying pan. The Indians prepared the fish by slitting the skin every 5 mm
(about 25 mm = 1 inch). Then herbs are rubbed into the slits. The fish were
delicious, according to the photographer, Dr. Herbert R. Axelrod.

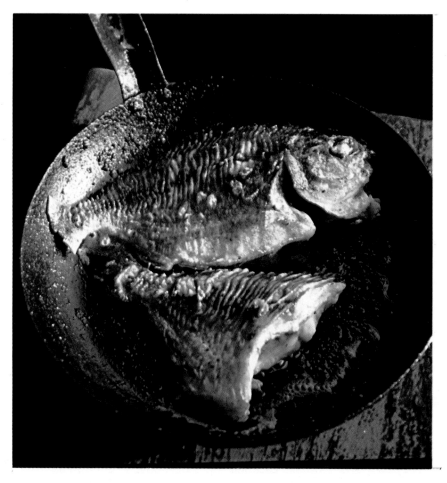

Suya Indian children assisting Harald Schultz and Dr. Axelrod in collecting small fishes. Photo by Harald Schultz.

are distributed over one immense single body of water. Now there is no shortage of food anymore. Everywhere one can see cheerful bathers, even children, in the waters that had been avoided before.

It would be naive to maintain that piranhas are perfectly harmless, yet there can be no doubt that it is high time to get this fish out of the "monster corner" once and for all.

In connection with all tales of adventure and suspense, one would do better to listen to the authority on South America already mentioned, Harald Schultz, who pokes fun at the atrocious stories about the danger of piranhas in a cynical anecdote:

> *When my father was fifteen years old, he fled from attacking Indians in a small, wobbly dugout canoe. The boat tipped over and he escaped by swimming, but when he*

*climbed out of the water he was a skeleton. Later nothing
like that could ever happen to him again!*

To depict piranhas as harmless, peaceful fish must be considered
just as naive and dangerous as building them up into monsters by
means of horror stories. As with so many things, here too the truth
lies within the often quoted "golden mean." Far too many factors
(not all obvious) can play a part in an attack by piranhas. Apart from
depending on the seasons and the seasonal changes in the water
level, the total food supply in the water, and the spawning periods,
aggressive behavior seems to be bound up with other factors or factor complexes connected with the water chemistry.

Attacks have occurred, are occurring, and will continue to occur
in the future, and nobody is able to make reliable predictions in that
respect; however, exaggerated scaremongering is absolutely inap-
propriate.

A young Caboclo boy on the Rio Negro has just harpooned a *Cichla
ocellaris* that was "drugged" with *timbo* poison. Photo by Dr. Herbert R.
Axelrod.

Piranhas in Myths, Rites, and in the Everyday Life of South American Indians

Alexander von Humboldt describes a special custom in the frequently flooded woodland and wet savannah zone of the Orinoco. In these regions, where burial of the dead is impossible during many months of the year because of flood waters, the *caribes* (piranhas) are assigned a cultural-mythical role as undertakers. The Guarani Indians, for instance, wrap their dead tightly in nets of a coarse mesh and let the piranahs, which occur there in large numbers, prepare the bodies for the actual funeral. When the piranhas have removed all the flesh from the bones, the nets are taken out of the water. The skeletons are then dried, sometimes colored with the red juice of the onoto plant (*Bixa orellana*), and adorned with all kinds of feathers. Finally they are given a place of honor in a high-lying spot or in the gable of a pole-and-thatch hut.

Piranhas are of importance in the life of not just Indian tribes in the Orinoco range. Numerous authors report independently that among the Indian tribes of the Amazon the piranhas—or their jaws—have in a variety of ways come to an important place in the life of these primitive groups, both in everyday living and in ritual. To some extent this continues today.

The Tucuna Indians, and likewise the Aweti of the Xingu headwaters, decorate their dancing masks with piranha teeth. Wooden masks with woven bast sleeves are painted by the Aweti with a specific piranha pattern, according to Schmidt, writing in 1905. This pattern is meant to symbolize the sharp and pointed sets of teeth of the piranhas. The exact cultural purpose of these masks is not known, however.

When visiting the Bakairi tribe on his journey from 1900 to 1901, Schmidt noted a larger number of painted wooden fish that the Indians wore on their heads as dancing decorations. A stick pushed through the belly served to fasten these imitation fish to additional headgear that was kept in position on the dancer's head by means of woven bands. The wooden fish were produced by the Indians in imitation of the piranha and in some cases perhaps also of the pacu (*Metynnis* sp.). Here, too, the exact cultural significance has unfortunately remained unknown. It would seem likely, however, that dancing with the wooden fish was connected with fishing. Perhaps it was intended to ensure a successful catch or to celebrate one.

Dancing masks with sets of piranha teeth. These were made by the Aweti Indians. After Schmidt, 1905, colored by John Quinn.

Apart from the symbolic cultural existence of piranhas in the folklore of the South American Indians, the piranha's jaws especially have their place in the ordinary everyday life of the primitive Indians as a practical commodity and as a tool. Above all, the lower jaw with its sharp teeth is used for shaving off the hair of the head, for sharpening thin blowgun darts, and for cutting all sorts of things. Even today, many Indian tribes of Brazil still refer to a pair of scissors (imported from Europe) as "piranha," since in function these have largely replaced the natural tool.

Indians who hunt with blowguns use the jaws of the piranha for yet another interesting purpose. When prey is within range (30 m or 100 feet), a dart about 30 cm (12 inches) long, matchstick-thin, and cut from the rib of a dry palm-leaf, is carefully pulled out of the bamboo quiver. After the hunter has wrapped some cotton-like kapok around the blunt end of the dart or "tsenac" for sealing and flight stabilization, he takes a piranha jaw from his belt and with the sharp, small teeth, cuts a deep notch into the wood above the brown tip of the dart that has been dipped into curare. This barb resists dislodging by the wounded animal. The Indians obtain the

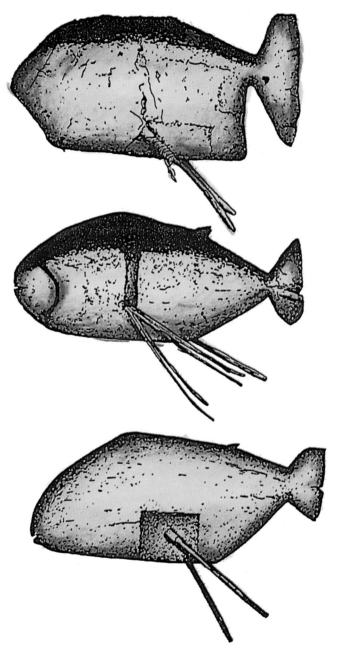

Wooden fish resembling piranhas were worn on the heads of Bakairi Indians during dancing rituals. Colored by John Quinn.

notorious paralyzing poison for their darts from the bark of plants of the genus *Strychnos*. The well-known alkaloid strychnine is derived from the seeds of *Strychnos* species, the East Indian tree *Strychnos nux-vomica*. After insertion into the blowgun follows the powerful, virtually silent shot. Birds are generally killed by the mere impact of the dart. Because of their higher body temperature, the poison on the dart also has a very rapid effect, since it quickly becomes distributed by the circulation of the blood.

In mammals, for example monkeys, it takes longer for the curare to take effect because it acts as a depressant of the respiratory muscles. Also, the poison has this effect only if it can act on the prey for long enough. Often it actually happens that monkeys immediately react by pulling the painful dart out of the wound. Any attempt by the animals to rid themselves of the troublesome dart, however, results in the latter breaking off at the intended point prepared for this purpose with the aid of the piranha jaw. The tip remains lodged under the skin and death occurs after a few minutes.

Indians throughout Brazil use certain vines from which they derive poison for fishing. They call this *timbo*. Photos in this series by Harald Schultz.

Since human beings emigrated from North America to South America about 12,000 (some say 40,000) years ago, their way of life has changed only little, at least in the vast, often inaccessible jungle regions. They catch fish with nets and rod and line, they shoot them with bow and arrow in the shallow water, or drive them to the surface with a poison derived from plants. The Waika Indians beat and squash pieces of certain lianas (e.g., *Jacquinia barbasco*) for this purpose. When the juice is exuded, the barbasco poison it contains

The vines are soaked in water and bashed. They have a soapy affect on the water as you can see from the bubbles floating on the surface. Photo of Yaruma Indians by Harald Schultz.

prevents the fish from utilizing the vital oxygen from the water. The fish come to the surface in a semi-anesthetized state and can be scooped up with baskets. There is no danger of stocks being depleted, since any unneeded fish are left in the river. Once the effect of the poison has worn off, the fish swim away without having come to any harm. Since piranhas are particularly easy to catch at virtually any time, they constitute a source of nourishing animal protein for the fishing tribes of Indians that must not be underestimated. They are valuable foodfish and practically always at the Indians' disposal.

These Karaja Indians, from the Rio Araguaia, Brazil, were organized by Dr. Axelrod to collect food and scientific specimens from an intermittent lake formed by the extremely low water conditions on the lower Rio Araguaia. The lake was about 6 feet (2 meters) deep in the center. The Indians were stationed in the lake with special "platforms" upon which to bash their *timbo* fish poison. The Spanish name for this poison is *barbasco*. The Indians were very successful using these platforms, but when Axelrod re-visited them some years later they had stopped using *timbo* altogether and couldn't remember why they stopped as civilization had caught up with them.

Piranha Biology

Since scientific classification, or systematics, is based almost entirely on the physical characteristics of a fish, some knowledge of the external and internal structure of piranhas is essential. This chapter is, therefore, intended as a survey of the most important physical characteristics and sensory capacities of piranhas that determine their modes of behavior, including feeding habits and reproduction.

Body Shape

The characteristic shape of the body is of importance not only as a clue for identification; it also provides information about the habits of a fish, since it always evolves in adaptation to the natural environment. The body shape of almost all piranhas is high-backed, more or less stocky, and strongly compressed laterally, which clearly indicates that they live in slow-flowing and stagnant waters. The head is relatively large, with a steep profile. The keel formed by enlarged scales and more or less extending along the midline of the belly is toothed like a saw. It is to this "saw" that the whole piranha family, Serrasalmidae (saw salmon), owes its name. External sex differences are not discernible. Often the male is of a slightly more slender build. A reliable differentiation of the sexes tends to be extremely difficult, however.

Fins

The fins, usually in combination with the air bladder, enable the fish to control all their movements. Being conspicuous distinguishing marks, they can serve as important aids to classification.

Every piranha has both paired and unpaired fins. They are named after the areas of the body in which they are inserted and, with the exception of the adipose fin, consist of rays with folds of thin skin (fin membrane) between them. Paired fins are the pectoral fins, which are inserted behind the gills, and the small ventral fins, attached on the abdomen, behind the pectorals. The unpaired (vertical) fins consist of the long-lobed anal fin that lies between the anus and the caudal peduncle; the caudal (or tail) fin, which has only a shallow notch; the dorsal fin; and the well-developed adipose fin behind it. The latter, not supported by rays, clearly marks all piranhas as characins. In front of the dorsal fin there is a small spine.

Scales and Coloration

As is the case with most fishes, the body of the piranhas is covered by the scales so characteristic of fishes. The individual scales are small horny plates developed from the skin. Each scales lies within a pocket of the skin and usually is covered by the epidermis (outer layer of the skin). The cycloid (round) scales of the piranhas are small, elastic, pliable, and set in the skin like the tiles on a roof, arranged in horizontal and vertical rows. They form an effective barrier against infection and foreign bodies. Above the scales lies a layer of skin that secretes copious mucus. Attacks and scratches constantly result in the loss of scales. This loss is harmless, however, since the scales regenerate quickly.

The scale formulas are of importance in systematics and are arrived at by counting the horizontal and vertical scale rows. Counting the scales of the lateral line gives an idea of the total number of vertical rows. The number of horizontal rows is found by counting the often oblique rows above and below the lateral line to as far as the origins of the dorsal and ventral fin bases respectively. The values thus obtained represent the desired scale counts.

A superficial glance at the scales is sufficient to notice a number of conspicuous concentric lines or circuli that run parallel with the edge. These are the growth rings that can be used to determine the age of a fish.

Apart from their protective value, the scales may also be a decisive factor as regards the coloration of a fish. Generally speaking, they themselves do not actually produce the color. Rather, the color is created by many pigment-containing cells—the chromatophores—in the skin in which the scales are embedded. If numerous cells with red pigment lie close together, the area concerned will look red. In many freshwater fishes the distribution of red helps members of the same species to recognize one another. In the piranhas, it occurs either in the form of eye color (*Serrasalmus spilopleura,* for instance) or as the coloration of the underside and abdomen (*Serrasalmus nattereri, S. notatus*). Some chromatophores are stimulated by light, which makes them expand and contract, thus causing color changes linked to the alternation of day and night. I observed color changes of that kind in *Serrasalmus nigricans*. Young specimens always showed a considerably darker coloration at night. Thus, coloration is the result of a biochemical process

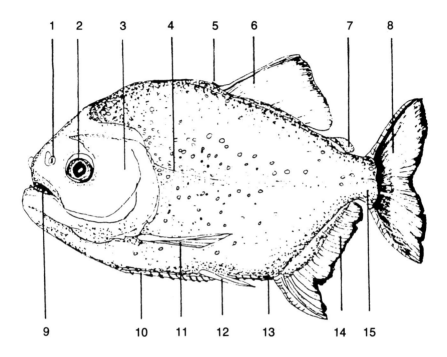

THE MOST IMPORTANT EXTERNAL PARTS OF A PIRANHA
1. The nostril or nasal aperture. 2. The eye. 3. The gill cover. 4. The lateral line. 5. The small spine. 6. The dorsal fin. 7. The adipose fin. 8. The tail or caudal fin. 9. The mouth. 10. The ventral keel. 11. The pectoral fin. 12. The pelvic fin. 13. The anal pore. 14. The anal fin. 15. The caudal peduncle.

that is dependent to some extent on health and mood as well as the environment. In some cases, an individual's age can be a factor of considerable significance. In the species *S. notatus,* the bright red color on the underside and the black spot on the flank noticeably fade with increasing age and size. Sacrificed piranhas of the same species that we preserved in formalin solution in Venezuela completely lost their characteristic bright red color within a mere two weeks or so, whereas the black spot on the flank remained.

Like numerous other species of fishes found in forests and jungles, many species of piranhas are characterized by a conspicuous metallic iridescence on a large number of their scales. This is caused by crystals (such as guanine) deposited in the scales and the refraction of light entering the crystals. It is highly probable that in loamy, cloudy tropical waters iridescence serves the purpose of species-recognition. Old specimens of various species of piranhas (*S. nattereri*, for example) can be so iridescent as to be justly referred to as "gold-dust piranhas."

Skeleton, Musculature, and Locomotion

Since the body weight is carried by the water, the main function of the skeleton is to support the whole musculature and provide a base to which the muscles can be attached. Further, it protects the brain and other vital organs by enclosing them.

The fully developed skeleton of the piranhas, like that of all bony fishes, allows one to draw conclusions about their habits. As compared with the delicate, thin skeleton of slow bottom-dwelling fishes, theirs can be described as being robust in build. This characteristic enables the piranhas to make quick and strong swimming movements. The musculature on each side of the trunk, which has the function of facilitating movement, is constructed of a series of narrow bundles of muscle (myomeres) arranged consecutively. The myomeres are complicated structures, like paper bags that have been put inside each other. Each consists of a dorsal and a ventral mass separated by connective tissue. It is by these septa of connective tissue, which show up as chevrons on the body muscle, that the musculature is attached to the vertebral column.

The swimming movement is snake-like and performed primarily by the strong lateral body muscles in conjunction with the caudal fin. None of the other fins are of any real importance in locomotion, and during fast swimming they are often folded close to the body. The paired fins generally are used only for steering and as stabilizers.

Teeth

The lower jaw in particular is big and immensely powerful, which contributes to the bulldog-like appearance of many older specimens. Strong muscles and tendons ensure the optimal functioning of the piranha's teeth. Hidden behind the lips there is an impressively large, extremely pointed, and razorblade-sharp dentition.

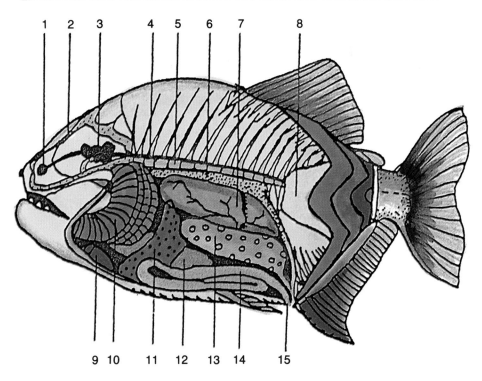

THE MOST IMPORTANT INTERNAL PARTS OF A PIRANHA
1. Olfactory bulb. 2. Skull. 3. Brain. 4. Spinal cord. 5. Spinal (vertebral) column.
6. Kidney. 7. Swim bladder. 8. Muscle section. 9. Heart. 10. Gills. 11. Liver. 12.
Stomach. 13. Sex organ. 14. Intestine. 15. Anal pore. Colored by John Quinn.
The drawing above can be compared to this piranha that was sliced open
carefully by Dr. Herbert R. Axelrod and then photographed by him.

In some species (*Serrasalmus rhombeus, S. spilopleura*) each side of the upper jaw is equipped with two parallel curved rows of teeth, the outer one (6 teeth) situated on the intermaxillary bone, the inner one (5-7 small teeth) on the palatine bones. The lower jaw, on the other hand, possesses merely a single curved row of 14 teeth on each side.

Because of their extremely powerful dentition, piranhas are able to cause serious injuries or death even to larger warm-blooded animals. Even a young piranha 15 cm (6 inches) in length has teeth that are 4 mm (1/6 inch) long!

Digestive Organs

The large mouth is followed by a spacious pharynx. The muscular gullet (esophagus) runs into the stomach without there being any conspicuous demarcation between the two. A constriction of the stomach (duodenum) indicates the beginning of the small intestine, which forms several loops and coils and extends almost to the anus. After passing through a very short rectum, which is barely distinguishable from the small intestine, the waste products are excreted through the anus. Salivary glands are not present. From the oral cavity to the anus, mucous glands can be found in the whole of the digestive tract. The liver is large and has a high fat content. There is no gallbladder.

Respiratory Organs

Inside openings (gill slits or clefts) between the pharynx and body wall lie the internal gills, the respiratory organs that take up dissolved oxygen from the water. The gills are composed of thin, reddish skin plates (gill lamellae) that are highly vascularized and protected from the outside by a gill cover (operculum).

During the process of respiration, the water flows through the open mouth into the pharynx (oral cavity). After the mouth has closed the water is forced out over the gills. If there is a shortage of oxygen in the water, piranhas, like many other species of fishes, come to the surface for gulps of air to increase the oxygen content of the water they have taken in. Toward the end of a drought, the "gurgling rings" produced by the fish gasping for air in the loam-yellow lagoons and the slowly crawling tributaries of the Orinoco were heard by us deep into the night.

Some species of fishes, such as eels, have adapted to the great shortage of oxygen in their habitats by their ability to breathe

Serrasalmus rhombeus collected and photographed by Dr. Herbert R. Axelrod in Brazil. The chewed-up fins resulted from netting dozens of specimens in a single net haul. The frightened fish snapped at anything that touched them. Not a single piranha in the haul of about 150 fish was undamaged. This was the best specimen. All of the piranhas in the haul were this same species.

through the skin as well as by means of the gills. The oxygen budget of many tropical waters makes it seem likely that numerous species of fishes that occur there also have the ability to take in oxygen through the skin. Where piranhas are concerned, this has not been shown, however.

Air Bladder

Fins enable the fish to exercise control over its movements, but the ability to remain suspended and virtually motionless in the water is given to the fish by the air bladder. This is situated above the gastro-intestinal tract under the spine and is used to register the changing water pressure (i.e., as a hydrostatic apparatus). By increasing and decreasing the amount of gas it contains, the air bladder allows the fish to adapt its specific gravity to that of the water surrounding it. In this way the fish can swim effortlessly at any depth. The gas inside the air bladder is similar to atmospheric air in composition. It is produced by a gas gland situated inside the air bladder. Excess gas is disposed of either via a tube (the ductus pneumaticus) that connects the air bladder with the gullet or by means of a small organ, situated inside the main chamber of the air bladder, that absorbs gas. This adjustment in pressure always proceeds slowly, and a voluntary contraction is not possible. In fish rapidly brought to the surface from a great depth the air bladder either becomes severely enlarged or it bursts.

As in numerous other species of fishes, in the piranhas the air bladder also serves as a resonator for sound produced either by the expulsion of gas or by two bones of the shoulder girdle rubbing against each other. The significance of the sounds still requires a satisfactory explanation. What is striking, however, is that many species of fishes, particularly those living in cloudy tropical waters such as gouramis and catfishes, are able to produce sounds that can be quite loud. It seems reasonable to interpret these as communicative sounds necessitated by limited visibility under water. Newly caught piranhas and catfishes utter sounds like warning cries, as do piranhas cornered in the aquarium with a net. The sounds emitted range from a whistling burr and a hissing of higher frequencies to a deep croaking. The noises made by piranhas are perhaps most aptly described as a "light croaking." Gouramis also croak.

The Venezuelans maintain that this croaking also serves as a "piranha alert" for river-dwelling and bathing Indians. The well-known botanist and tropical ecologist Prof. Dr. Volkmar Vareschi describes in an anecdote how, during an expedition to the Orinoco, he wanted to bathe unmolested by piranhas in the deep pool of a rapids, when suddenly he heard the characteristic croaking of the piranhas. Having hastily surfaced and shot out of the water, he searched for the supposed cause of the noise, and it was only after this process had been repeated several times that he realized he had been running away from his own stomach rumbles that had been amplified by the rocks!

Heart and Circulatory System

The heart lies immediately behind the gill arches in front of the shoulder girdle. It is inside a sac (the pericardium) separated from the abdominal cavity by a vertical septum. The heart is composed of two sections: the nonmuscular expansion of the bulbus arteriosus with only a single pair of valves, and the muscular chamber of the heart (ventricle).

By contractions of the heart, the blood is forced into the first (ascending) part of the aorta, whence paired lateral branches lead to every gill arch. The vessels that supply the gills with blood grow increasingly smaller and finer, terminating in the capillary network of the gill lamellae. After having taken up oxygen, the blood flows through the efferent vessels of the gills into the vessels that supply the head and body (carotid artery and descending aorta). Arteries lead to the individual internal organs and supply them with blood that is rich in oxygen.

The purification of the blood is carried out by the kidneys and liver. The oval red blood corpuscles measure 0.005–0.023 mm. There is also a lymphatic circulation with a network of vessels.

Dried out after they have been soaked in formalin, and then varnished, souvenir piranhas are a big business in Brazil, where 50,000 a year are prepared for export and local consumption.

Internal Secretions and Excretion

A few glands discharge their secretions (e.g., hormones) into the blood that flows through them or into the fluid of the abdominal cavity in general, so secretions can reach all the individual organs and tissues. The secretions, most of which are of a complex chemical structure, take effect in very small quantities.

Important Glands and Their Functions

Thyroid Gland: Regulation of the metabolism.

Thymus: Influences growth and the development of the gonads, for instance. Produces T-lymphocytes.

Pancreas: One portion produces digestive enzymes, the other— the islets of Langerhans—produces insulin, necessary for keeping the blood sugar at a constant level. The "islets" are quite distinct in structure and position from the rest of the gland.

Adrenal Cortices: Secrete corticosterone, a chemical of vital importance in respiration. Adrenalin produced inside the medulla has a stimulating effect on the heartbeat rate (for example) and thereby raises the blood pressure and affects the lumen of the blood vessels.

Pituitary Gland: Secretes a variety of hormones that influence growth, fat and carbohydrate metabolism, and the development of the sex organs. Its hormones also affect other glands of the body (thyroid, pancreas, adrenal glands, etc).

Gonads: Produce gametes (sexual reproductive cells) and hormones and regulate sexual activity. They are controlled largely by the pituitary body (hypophysis).

The Kidneys: (Mesonephric in the adult), lie along the vertebral column and extend from behind the head to the posterior end of the abdominal cavity, and function as excretory organs. The waste is eliminated through two tubes, the ureters, which are joined distally and open behind the anus. The principal breakdown products are uric acid and ammonia.

Nervous System and Sense Organs

The **central nervous system** consists of: 1) forebrain, diencephalon, midbrain, cerebellum, and medulla oblongata; 2) the nerve centers extending into the spinal cord and into the different organs, including the sense organs.

All environmental stimuli received by the sense organs are registered by the brain and can trigger specific reactions controlled by different nerves. Many instinctive reactions are the result of a reflex-like process whereby the spinal cord acts as the central trigger. In an experiment with eels, the brain was almost completely severed from the spinal cord. Nevertheless, the animals made the same natural snake-like movements as before the operation. This was clear proof that movement, too, is controlled largely by the spinal cord.

In the following, the main sense organs shall be discussed.

In the Rio Abacaxis, which flows into the Rio Madeira, Dr. Axelrod collected a new subspecies of discus, *Symphysodon discus willischwartzi*. In this blackwater river it was the first *Symphysodon discus* ever found south of the Amazon. Axelrod also found a piranha in this blackwater river that closely resembles *Serrasalmus (Pygocentrus) manueli* Fernandez-Yepez and Ramirez, 1967.

The Lateral Line

The lateral line can be clearly seen with the naked eye as a thin line extending along both sides of the body from the gill cover (operculum) to the caudal peduncle. It forms the principal course of a canal and groove system that divides into three branches as it reaches the head. One branch runs along the lower jaw, the second below the eye, and the third above the eye. On the head, these grooves and canals lie inside the dermis but more or less open to the water. On the body they are covered with scales and maintain contact with the water by means of special pores in the scales. Into the mucus-filled canals project the sensory bristles of the sensory cells, mechanoreceptors sensitive to pressure waves. They detect pressure waves produced in the water and thereby alert the fish to vibrations of any kind. The wriggling of a sick fish is registered as quickly and accurately by means of this "long-range tactile sense" as is the motion of other moving objects. It is highly probable that the lateral line also enables the fish to recognize members of the same species by their characteristic frequency of motion. Pressure waves produced by courtship displays and by mock fights between rival males are detected by it as well. Another function of the lateral line is to help the fish to keep its balance. In turbid water it serves as an important aid to orientation, since obstacles are noticed at an early stage through reflected pressure waves alone.

Smell

The olfactory organ represents one of the first sense organs to appear in the history of vertebrate evolution, and consequently it is very well developed in almost all fishes. The paired nostrils, consisting of mucous-tissue-lined pits, lie on both sides of the head above the snout. The apertures of these nasal pits are divided into anterior and posterior openings by a skin septum. Having entered by this opening, the water flows past the greatly folded olfactory mucous membrane lining (the folding increases surface area) covered with sensory cells that communicate with the brain via the olfactory nerve and the olfactory lobes.

Many authors have mentioned the fantastic sense of smell enjoyed by sharks. According to Steuben, they are able to detect blood and fish oil in a dilution of 1:1,500,000 and pursue a trail of scent with unflagging resoluteness.

Piranhas, too, seem to have an extraordinarily acute sense of smell. The simplest of experiments are sufficient to prove this. In a tank of 200 liters (52 gallons) capacity, I once kept a piranha 22 cm (10 inches) in length. Over the years it had either devoured or outlived all the other members of its shoal. When the animal was hungry, a single drop of blood or meat juice placed in the tank was enough to cause it to become visibly agitated. Several drops induced the piranha to swim toward the supposed prey. This was always followed by a phase of excited swimming about at great speed. Pieces of meat lying on the bottom were invariably approached and picked up in a very purposeful manner, and bits of food hidden among dense vegetation were always found very quickly.

Serrasalmus nattereri collected and photographed by Dr. Herbert R. Axelrod.

Reports furnish the information that the smell of blood can attract large numbers of piranhas within a very short time.

Taste

The organs of taste consist of small bud-shaped structures (taste buds) that, although distributed over the whole body of the fish, are particularly numerous inside the mouth and pharynx. They are sensory cells enveloped by protective cells and project from the outer layer of the skin (epidermis) like buds. Apart from their chemical function as taste-receptors, these cells also react to variations in temperature.

Collecting piranhas, as well as many other fishes, requires a team effort. A large seine is spread across a shallow stream. There is a man at each end of the seine. Two other men move from upstream, beating the water as they proceed toward the seine. Photo by Dr. Herbert R. Axelrod.

Hearing

The labyrinth of the bony fishes, which lies entirely inside the skull, constitutes the internal ear and the organ of balance at one and the same time. Experimental destruction of the labyrinth results in the fish's movements becoming uncontrolled. The labyrinth consists of semicircular canals filled with fluid and containing calcareous concretions known as otoliths. By means of a chain of small ossicles (the Weberian apparatus), the labyrinth is connected to the air bladder, and the latter's variations in pressure can be detected by the ear. (The Weberian apparatus is absent in higher bony fishes.) Countless experiments with bony fishes such as minnows and catfishes confirm that their hearing capacity is excellent. Since piranhas themselves actually produce sounds, it may be assumed that they, too, can hear very well.

When swimming, fishes normally produce characteristic sound-waves of low frequency. Since sound vibrations spread four to five times as quickly under water as they do in the atmosphere, wriggling injured fish are most certainly identified as such by piranhas by the change in frequency. More detailed information on the hearing capacity of piranhas would result from further research.

The Eyes

The relatively large eyes of the piranhas, in their structure similar to those of other higher vertebrates, have a hard, spherical lens that does not change shape. The cornea is flattish and barely convex. Being typical fish eyes, they neither move nor possess true eyelids. Tear glands are absent, too, since the surfaces are bathed by the water. Via optic nerves, all visual images are transmitted to the brain and there coordinated. The eye is perfectly adapted for close-up vi-

The seine is very deep, about 12' (4 m), so that it develops a belly that prevents fishes from jumping out of it. The seine is closed and then dragged onto the bank, where the fishes are examined. Photo by Dr. Herbert R. Axelrod.

The fishermen carefully pull in the seine by pulling on the bottom line, the idea being to trap the fishes in the submerged pocket of the bulging seine. In most cases, the piranhas chew up the seine and each other in the process. Photo by Dr. Herbert R. Axelrod.

sion, and at rest it is short-sighted. An adaptation to greater distances is achieved by the lens being displaced in the direction of the retina by means of lens muscle attached to the back of the lens.

Thanks to the position and shape of the eyes, piranhas, like most fishes, survey a very wide field of view. To a limited extent they even are able to perceive movements that go on behind them. This means that the fish become aware of possible danger at an early stage and thus have an increased chance of escaping. The ability to look all around further ensures that the movements of any kind of prey do not go unnoticed either.

Anteriorly, the broad visual fields of the two eyes intersect. Only in this narrow field of intersection does the piranha have stereoscopic vision. If the fish wants to subject a potential prey to closer scrutiny, it turns toward it and thus brings it into the range of intersection. Before an attack can take place the distance needs to be estimated, which requires stereoscopic vision.

THE VISUAL FIELD OF THE PIRANHA This pattern illustrates the range where the vision from both eyes can focus on a single subject. The dark area shows the very limited stereoscopic field of vision.

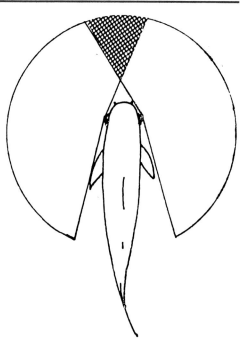

What astonishing feats the piscine eye is capable of was demonstrated by experiments with minnows and perches, for example. Not only did the fishes recognize geometric figures, but they even noticed differences in size of as little as 1 mm (1/25 inch). Color vision is very acute, too. It was possible to train minnows to distinguish between 20 different shades of color between 700 and 370 nanometers. These tests established that even ultraviolet light (below 397nm) can be perceived with the eyes.

As yet no experimental data on limits of vision are available where piranhas are concerned. However, since the eye of the piranha is very similar in structure to that of the minnows, it must be assumed that the piranha's visual performance is equally good.

Reproduction

In the male, the testes have spermatic ducts exiting directly. In the female, the eggs reach the body cavity after rupture of the ovarian membrane and are discharged to the outside through the genital pore behind the anus.

As yet no satisfactory reports are available on the exact onset of sexual maturity in piranhas. It looks as though there is a spawning period before the rainy season in April/May and possibly a second one in late summer. Prior to spawning the general aggressiveness of the piranhas increases considerably, and members of the same species are bitten more frequently. In public aquaria, repeated losses occur due to extremely excited, ripe piranhas attacking one another. Submerged plants that get in the way are almost completely bitten off and spawning pits (nests) are made. The pairs already defend their spawning territory at this stage! The intensified aggression in the parents continues for some time after spawning.

Color changes during the spawning period can be observed in *S. nattereri,* for instance. Overall, the animals grow slightly lighter in color, the red color in the abdominal region becomes more intense, and the general iridescence greatly diminishes.

In the first photographically documented spawning of a piranha, the foremost Japanese aquarist, Hiroshi Azuma, was able to capture the spawning of *Serrasalmus nattereri.* The fish prepare a nest, almost like birds! They then align their bodies (facing page) right over the nesting site. Photos by Hiroshi Azuma.

Gedaschke described the spawning process observed with regard to *Serrasalmus rhombeus* in an aquarium at Duisburg Zoo: *. . . toward the evening, the love play so characteristic of characins could be seen once again; the egg-laying was a protracted process lasting from 7 p.m. to 10 p.m.* The female deposited the spawn near a root among dense moss (*Fontinalis* sp.). Afterward the spawn was fiercely defended by the parents. Gery writes about the reproduction of piranhas: *It is probable that, like more highly developed fishes, they practice brood-care.* The truth of this assumption was

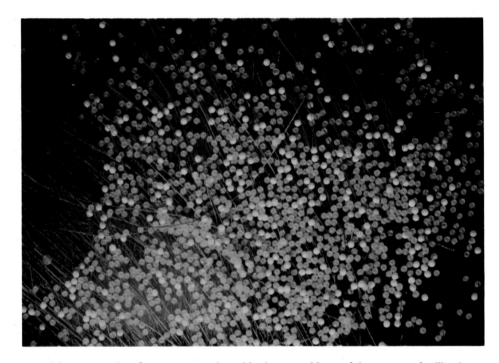

A large quantity of eggs are produced in the nest. Many of them are unfertilized and become opaque white within a few hours (depending upon the water temperature). The complete story was reported in *Tropical Fish Hobbyist* magazine. Photo by Hiroshi Azuma.

confirmed by observations made by Honegger (Zurich, 1971) in respect to *Serrasalmus nattereri*. It would seem likely that it is equally true where the other species of piranhas are concerned.

Depending on the water temperature, the fry hatch after two to three days. They lose their yolk sac after four to five days at a size of about 7 mm (¼ inch).

A closeup of a developing piranha egg. The breeders protect the nest and the eggs. Photo by Hiroshi Azuma.

Feeding Habits

After resorption of the yolk sac at the age of about four days, the young piranhas have to start looking for food, so now the predacious life begins in earnest for them. Tiny crustaceans and protozoans constitute the first "hunted" food. Growing rapidly, the fish then turn primarily to water insects, small worms, and mosquito larvae. By the time they measure 25 mm (1 inch), they attack smaller fish and, increasingly, weaker members of their own species as well. As the piranhas get bigger, their aggression and cannibalism clearly can be seen to intensify. Fish form the staple food of growing and fully grown piranhas. The killing and devouring of warm-blooded animals must be regarded as exceptional.

Often, and with some relish, piranhas as a whole are cited as the prime example when it comes to animal voraciousness. This may be due to a naive mistaken belief that, simplified, can be expressed as follows: the more dangerous and aggressive is an animal, the greater and more immoderate are the amounts of food it devours. As is so often the case, reality is altogether different! Droescher in 1979 described experiments carried out in the aquarium by the behavioral scientist Richard M. Fox. In one of his experiments, the latter put 25 goldfish—all of roughly the same size—into a large aquarium as live food for two piranhas (*S. nattereri*) that were about 10 cm (4 inches) long. Instead of indulging in a wild orgy of mass killings, the two piranhas contented themselves with killing just one fish per day and eating it between them. This, in fact, corresponds entirely to the normal daily food requirements. Another interesting fact was observed by Fox: within a short time, all the remaining goldfish had every one of their fins bitten off by the piranhas. This meant that the goldfish, while still alive, were quite unable to swim normally. Usually they were reeling around helplessly in the water with the head downward. In this way the two young piranhas had managed to secure for themselves a food supply that was unable to escape and could be reached easily at any time.

That the reeling movements of a sick or injured fish have a powerful trigger-effect on the aggression of piranhas and other predatory fishes is a fact that has been observed often and can be seen again and again. This makes it seem all the more surprising that the food-fishes that were wriggling and reeling all the time were not attacked by the piranhas more than once a day. It must be assumed, therefore, that in a state of satiation, the wriggling movements, although still perceived by the sense organs, no longer have the immediate trigger-effect that brings about an attack.

The teeth of the piranhas are extremely pointed and as sharp as a razor blade. As opposed to predacious fishes that swallow their prey whole, to the piranhas the size of their prey is quite immaterial: they are always able to cut off a morsel of food that fits into their mouths. In this respect, the feeding behavior of the piranhas is very similar to that of the sharks, and among freshwater fishes it is undoubtedly unique. Just like sharks, piranhas that have made their sudden attack and sunk their teeth into the prey can be seen to make characteristic shaking movements that serve to tear out the morsel. The shaking movements are extremely vigorous and cause the whole animal to tremble violently. Afterward, the fish swims off making swallowing movements. When the process of swallowing has been completed, it rapidly swims back, in an arc, to pounce on the prey again. Often the piranhas get so intoxicated by the food and so excited that they take bites out of each other's fins or bodies as well or, in some

A two-week-old piranha fry with the yolk sac almost completely absorbed. It measures about 9-10 mm in length. Photo by Hiroshi Azuma.

cases, launch a full-scale attack on one another.

Although some specimens in the aquarium show a tendency to form territories, juvenile piranhas generally live and hunt in shoals in fairly close association with one another. The question as to whether this applies to fully grown piranhas as well is still awaiting a satisfactory answer. The reason for this is self-evident: observations in the open waters of the sea are comparatively easy to carry out, whereas diving in the warm, loamy "broth" of a tropical river teeming with piranhas clearly presents rather more of a problem.

Experiments with piranhas kept in the aquarium, carried out by Prof. H. Mankl from Freiburg revealed that fish prey are invariably hunted by a "gang" of several cooperating adult animals. After carefully creeping up to within at least 25 cm (10 inches), the first piranha shoots up and bites the tailfin off the fleeing fish. The next piranha cuts off the caudal peduncle, the third the anal region, etc.

A *Serrasalmus* species attacking a chunk of meat. It opens its mouth to the fullest and swims quickly to get a big mouthful, that it tears out neatly with its sharp teeth. Sharks have a very similar feeding attack. Photo by J. J. van Duinen.

The prey is thus carved up from behind into mouthfuls and dies within a few moments.

The hunting method just described indicates that the fish get together in smallish groups. That fully grown piranhas roam their natural habitat in larger shoals, as is often maintained, is fairly unlikely. Looking at the majority of reports available so far, the most realistic assumption would seem to be that they live in smallish associations. This does not, however, exclude the possibility that bigger prey (e.g., carrion) would within seconds attract masses of piranhas from a wider area. These would then form a feeding shoal and would disperse after having eaten their fill.

I personally was able to observe the hunting and feeding behavior of a large shoal of piranhas at feeding time at Duisburg Zoo, where about 50 piranha of varying age were being kept in a show tank of 4500 liters (1260 U.S. gallons) capacity.

Immediately after a living foodfish (in this case a rainbow trout measuring 30 cm [12 inches] in length) is put into the tank, the attack begins. Numerous piranhas turn toward the foodfish and hurry after it. Within fractions of seconds, one piranha has effortlessly bitten a walnut-sized piece of flesh out of the fleeing trout's back just behind the head. Extremely aggravated by hunting instinct and envy, the first group of attackers inflicts six deep, circular bite wounds on the trout. The bites are randomly distributed over the body, with the piranhas literally attacking from all sides. The lower abdominal region is torn open. Helpless, the trout manages one final instinctive attempt to escape. Then comes an almost perfectly synchronized attack by a second group of at least 20 to 25 adult and juvenile piranhas. Clouds of muscle fibers and bits of intestine and their contents form, penetrated by more and more piranhas. The number of animals that all attack at the same time rapidly grows so large that the remains of the foodfish disappear from view. Even the bottom of the tank is disturbed, and the water in the whole tank grows cloudy. The last clouds of dark intestinal contents and white muscle fibers whirl about as a few piranhas dart about in the turbid water, searching and snapping. After about 20 to 30 seconds, the whole spooky business is over, the intoxication with food gradually wears off, and the piranhas's movements grow slower and calmer again. There is nothing left of the trout.

There can be no doubt that the observation of such an attack by piranhas is one of those natural phenomena that leave an impression one will never forget.

Mimicry is not uncommon in fishes. It is always a question of whether the one that mimics seeks the advantage for aggression or whether the other fish seeks it for protection. The upper fish is the piranha *Serrasalmus notatus*, while the mimic on the bottom is the harmless *Colossoma bidens*. Does *S. notatus* imitate *C. bidens* in order to get close to prey? Or does *C. bidens* mix with schools of *S. notatus* for protection? Photo by Leo G. Nico.

Bite Inhibition

Being cannibalistic, piranhas sometimes attack members of their own species, but healthy animals appear to observe a kind of truce among themselves. This necessitates the recognition of members of the same species by the diagnostic characteristics of disc-shaped, shining bodies and characteristic species coloration. The presence of both these characteristics effectively inhibits the biting drive, although it does not prevent the biting that occurs when the fish are intoxicated with food and during spawning. Since some close relatives of the *Serrasalmus* species (such as *Myleus asterias*) are very similar in shape and coloration, they, too, remain unharmed, as a rule.

The well-known Venezuelan ichthyologist (scientist studying fishes) Prof. Dr. Mago-Leccia in 1978 referred to the species *Colossoma bidens,* which also belongs to the Serrasalmidae, as an example of almost perfect mimicry (camouflage and deception) by potential prey. To be safe from pursuit by its predacious cousins, this species has developed an almost perfect imitation of the body shape and coloration of the piranha *Serrasalmus notatus,* a species that is very common in the Orinoco.

Natural Enemies

In some ways their major natural enemy, man is constantly pursuing the piranhas, using all sorts of methods to catch them. In addition, piranhas in their natural habitat have cause to fear the Brazilian giant otter (*Teronura brasiliensis*), the largest otter on earth, up to 2.2 m (almost 7 feet) long (inclusive of the tail) and weighing up to 24 kg (53 pounds). Unfortunately the otter is becoming rarer all the time. Especially important predators are, above all, the caimans. Gerlach in 1950 cites an informative account of a shooting expedition by Krieg in 1948. He was hunting in the La Plata region and witnessed an attack by piranhas with an unexpected outcome. The excerpt from Krieg's report quoted here starts after he had shot a caiman and cut open the latter's flank on the shore:

> *A few minutes later masses of* palometas *(the local name for piranhas in the La Plata region), attracted by the blood in the water, had gathered around the dead caiman. Greedily they appeared to sink their teeth into the latter's open flank and tear out scraps of flesh and entrails. There was splashing and bubbling, darting and snatching going on in the warm water near the shore, and often one could see the sudden flash of a body as a fish jumped out of the water and then fell back in again with a splash. All this had the effect on the caimans of an alarm being sounded. A few swam up immediately, eyes above the water, and*

Piranhas of the same species seem to have a truce and rarely attack one another unless they are starving or one is wounded. Drawn by Yuri Kaverkin.

The photo above, plus the facing page photograph, proves that piranhas of the same species and approximately the same size can be kept together. Battles between healthy specimens of the same species are extremely rare. Photo above by Dr. Herbert R. Axelrod; photo on the facing page by Hans-Joachim Richter.

eagerly caught palometas *that were attacking the cadaver of their fellow caiman. As they snatched their prey, their bodies generally went into a vertical position, at right angles to the neck. Very few devoured the fish there and then. The majority, head raised, a wriggling fish between the teeth, found themselves a quieter spot nearby and there proceeded to consume their prey in peace.*

Piscivorous birds such as herons and cormorants form another group of natural enemies, although strictly speaking they constitute a real danger to piranhas only when the latter are still in the juvenile stage. A few species of river turtles (e.g., matamatas) may also attack young piranhas. The major decimation of sick and injured animals comes about as a result of cannibalism.

Among the most interesting piranha hunters, however, are undoubtedly the freshwater dolphins (*Inia*) that have evolved in the tropical Amazon and Orinoco.

During an *Inia* hunting expedition, the director of Duisburg Zoo, Dr. Gewalt, and his hunting team also came across piranhas. Standing in the water, the dolphin hunters were frequently tweaked through trouser-clad legs by piranhas. There were no injuries, however, except very minor ones to the hands when piranhas accidentally caught in the nets were put back into the water and naturally snapped about them. The hunting team from Duisburg fished for piranhas with rod and line. Peter Schulz, an employee at Duisburg Zoo, related that on more than one occasion freshly-caught piranhas lying on the river bank suddenly seemed to vanish without trace. The invisible culprits were soon discovered, however: they were birds of prey about the size of a falcon that quickly learned to seize even a piranha that was still wriggling on the line while being reeled in and rise up into the air with it. The team actually succeeded in filming this curiosity.

This is a seine haul in a piranha-infested lagoon. There are many small fishes mixed in with the small piranhas. Photo by Leo G. Nico.

Inia geoffrensis, the Amazonian freshwater dolphin or porpoise, is a piranha gourmet, almost specializing in eating them. Drawing from Marine Mammals of the World.

Range and Ecology

South America, with its immense river systems, constitutes the natural range of the piranhas. They occur in the Orinoco and Amazon as well as in the majority of their tributaries, in the rivers of Guyana, and in the Brazilian Rio Šao Francisco, as well as in the basins of the Rio Paraguay and the Rio Paraná. Not without good reason were these large bodies of water described as freshwater oceans by the first European explorers. The Amazon itself forms the largest river system on earth.

Whitewater Rivers

The majority of piranhas live in the so-called "whitewater rivers" of South America. These are rivers carrying loamy water with a great deal of fine material in suspension. Due to these mineral substances that cause the water to grow turbid (mainly fine silt and clays in granulations of 0.002 to 0.00002 millimeters), the rivers appear milky yellow-gray in color or, in areas with a laterite soil (tropical red loams) and especially when there is high water, reddish brown. One cubic meter (35 cubic feet) of such loamy rivers, to which the term "whitewater" barely applies anymore, may contain up to 1.5 kilograms (3¼ pounds) of mineral substances in suspension. On average, according to Lueling, a "normal" South American whitewater river carries 300 milligrams of dry substance per liter (3 parts in 10,000).

Most of the big whitewater rivers of South America are waters that come from the—geologically speaking—young Andes or their spurs. The residual soil is constantly being washed off by the rain and subsequently transported in rills, brooks, streams, and finally the rivers into the sea. Not only is the mineral content high, there is also a large proportion of hardeners and plant nutrients (salts, etc.). The development of a phytoplankton as a source of primary production is, however, impeded by weak and inadequate illumination and too strong a current.

According to measurements by Lueling (on April 19, 1967, with a white Secchi visibility disc), the Rio Madeira above Porto Velho, Rondonia, for example, had a visibility depth of only 16 centimeters (6½ inches). At a water depth of 5 centimeters (2 inches), 61% of the light from the surface was still present. At a depth of 30 centimeters (12 inches) this had diminished to 8%. Thus most of the water

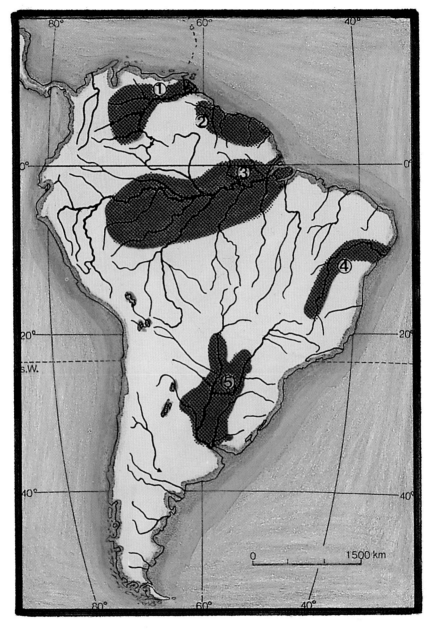

THE NATURAL RANGE OF THE PIRANHA.
Piranhas only exist in nature in South America. Regardless of the fears of many governments, piranha populations have never resulted from either accidental or deliberate introduction. The natural ranges of the piranhas are: **1.** The Orinoco range. **2.** The Guyana range. **3.** The Amazon range. **4.** The Rio Sao Francisco range. **5.** The Rio Paraguay and Rio Parana range.

in a whitewater river is dark or completely without light. This explains the paucity or absence of vegetable plankton and higher submersed plants. My own analyses of the water established that the pH tends to be neutral (6.5-7.5). The water temperatures remain almost constant between 27-29°C (81-84°F) in the Orinoco.

In the middle and lower courses, the channels of the whitewater streams are several kilometers (over a mile) wide as a rule. Consequently, depending on current and granulation, there is a striated deposition of suspended material near the edges. At the same time, according to Grzimek, enormous inshore lakes (up to 100 km or 60 miles in length and 40 kilometers or 24 miles in width) often get cut off from the main stream until the water level grows high again. The Spanish term for the marginal zone is *varzea*. In these lakes, such a vast proportion of the suspended material is deposited that sunlight is often able to filter through the warm water (27-35°C, 81-95°F) to a depth of several meters and so makes possible the growth of higher and lower plants, the prerequisite for a food chain leading up to predacious fishes like the piranhas.

The arapaima (*Arapaima gigas*) belongs to the Osteoglossidae (bony tongues) and, at a maximum weight of 120 kilograms (260 pounds) and a length of 2 to 2.5 meters (6½-8¼ feet), is the biggest freshwater fish on earth. It also lives and spawns in the *Varzeas.* These lakes on the edges of the rivers are full of life, harboring the greatest diversity of forms of nearly all groups of organisms, including the freshwater dolphin, *Inia.* Every species finds its own particular ecological niche here. Near the shore, the surface is often covered with various floating plants—the famous *Victoria regia* water lily, for instance. Typical white water streams are the Amazon, the Orinoco, the Madeira, the Paraná-Paraguay, and the Uruguay rivers.

Blackwater Rivers

The blackwater rivers rise in tropical forest swamps of the lowlands and slowly flow through extensive tree-clad plains. The roots of trees that are standing in the water, as well as rotting vegetable matter that has dropped down, extract oxygen, scarce enough as it is, from the blackwater. In blackwater rivers of the Orinoco, the ox-

Arapaima gigas with a Brazilian Indian. These are the largest freshwater fish in the world. Photo by Dr. Herbert R. Axelrod.

ygen content is as low as 0.003 ppm (parts per million). Because of this severe oxygen deficiency, organic material (leaves, branches, etc.) that falls into the water is only partially broken down or recycled by the few bacteria that occur here. Instead of the large humus molecules that are insoluble in water, only extremely short-lived, water-soluble pre-humic compounds are formed. Due to the frequent rains, these are quickly washed away from the characteristic

The Rio Abacaxis in Brazil is a blackwater river that periodically overflows its banks, killing all the trees it floods due to the very acid quality of the water. Photos by Hans-Joachim Richter.

The characteristic snow-white sandy beaches common to most black-water rivers. This is the Rio Negro far north in the town of San Gabriel. Photo by Dr. Herbert R. Axelrod.

snow-white sandy shores of the blackwater rivers.

Viewed through glass, blackwater resembles heavily diluted black tea. In the riverbed it appears dark brown to black—hence, of course, the name blackwater river or blackwater stream. There is visibility down to a depth of about 50 centimeters (20 inches) to 3 meters (10 feet) depending on how strongly the water is colored by humic substances. Because there is no erosive action, blackwater rivers carry virtually no mineral substances or dissolved salts at all. Furthermore, there is an extraordinary shortage of lime and other electrolytes; the trace elements here are calcium and magnesium (only of minimal conductivity).

Due to the large amounts of humic acids that are not being buffered by hardeners, blackwater is very acidic. In the main stream of the Rio Negro, pH values of around 4 were recorded. In its tributaries, the pH was found to be as low as 3.7. I personally recorded pH values of around 4.5-5 in the Rio Carrao and Rio Caroni near Canaima, Venezuela.

During the flood season from about December through April, the Rio Negro overflows its banks, enabling small fishes to spawn in safety. The local people must live in boats. Photo by Dr. Herbert R. Axelrod.

The Brazilian Rio Negro is the best example of a larger blackwater river. Without possessing any actual source, it rises from swampy palm groves in Colombia. Alongside the actual riverbed, the Rio Negro creates a floodplain in a valley many kilometers broad during the high-water period. At this time the water level may be as much as 10 meters (33 feet) above normal. The forest growing in this valley (*Igapo*), has completely adapted to this unusual habitat with its periodic floodings. The roots are almost constantly standing in water with very little oxygen, and even when totally flooded, perhaps for months, the trees do not lose their leaves.

High acidity and little light mean that photosynthesis, and hence the beginning of a food chain, is largely absent from blackwater rivers. Consequently, the number of animals that settle there is minimal. Only where whitewater flows in from the tributaries the living conditions for algae, bacteria, and, of course, fishes become more favorable. Lueling comments: *I feel certain that in most cases where our lists of piscine fauna supply the vague information 'Rio Negro,' the fish concerned had in fact been caught in that type of mixed water zone.*

Where blackwater and whitewater rivers mix, impressive revolving, cloud-like shapes are often described and photographed. The most famous and biggest of these mixed zones exists where the Rio Negro flows into the Amazon near Manaus. Until their final mixture, the dividing line between blackwater and whitewater can be followed for another 80 kilometers (48 miles) or so from Manaus down the Amazon! Piranhas also occur in this mixed water zone.

Clearwater Rivers

Clearwater rivers mostly have their origin in areas that are old geologically, evolving during the Paleozoic era. Since they are not able to wash particles in any significant amounts out of the granites or gneisses found there, their water is clear and translucent. For the

An aerial view of the Rio Negro as the river began receding in September. There are thousands of small islands that provide hiding places for many fishes. The white beaches are beginning to appear. Photo by Dr. Herbert R. Axelrod.

same reason they have virtually no sedimentary substances to deposit during flooding, nor do they form lakes on the edges. The riverbed never changes, even during periods of high water. Although the nutrient content is often comparatively low, their strong illumination (down to 7 meters or 23 feet and more!) ensures that clearwater rivers are full of plant and animal life. Apart from *Cabomba*, all sorts of submersed plants do extremely well there. In addition, so do an almost unimaginable quantity of small fishes—dwarf cichlids and characins of varying species, for instance.

The major variations in the water level—by up to 7 meters (23 feet)—that occur each year, and that a normal vegetation growing on the riverbank is not able to cope with, is also the reason why clearwater rivers such as the Rio Xingu and Rio Tapajos are accompanied by kilometer-long stretches of almost sterile, white sandy shores.

The pH values of the clearwater rivers can be anything between 5.5 and 7. When the current becomes less strong for a time, notably in the lower courses of the river, a massive proliferation of green

Below: Dr. Herbert R. Axelrod paddling up a previously un-mapped stream that contains muddy Amazon-type water. The igarape is near Tefe, Brazil. **Facing page:** A clearwater stream, about 3 feet (1 m) deep, containing many fishes hiding in the grassy overhang. Photo by Dr. Herbert R. Axelrod. Photo below by Harald Schultz.

algae, but most especially of blue algae of the genus *Anabaena,* can result in what is known as an algal bloom. Piranhas are rare and generally occur only in the cloudy regions where two rivers meet and clearwater and whitewater mix.

Adaptation and Function in the Ecosystem

As already mentioned, the variations in the water level of the rivers in the warm, humid tropics are often considerable despite constant rainfall. In the lower Amazon where the differences grow noticeably less, they still amount to something like 6 to 10 meters (20-33 feet), in the middle segment 10 to 16 meters (33-53 feet). The regular seasonal variations in rainfall also make themselves felt in its tributaries. The river then forms new inlets, ramifications, large lakes along the edges, and lagoons near the banks. Thus each incident of highwater is followed by changes in water depths and extent of the banks and at times of the individual arms of the river. Depressions that are parallel with the bank—and during highwater sometimes already fill up on their own accord due to the general increase in the level of the subsoil water—do not always dry up completely during the period with little rainfall. The same applies to the lakes on the edges and the depressions filled up by the river itself.

During the rainy season (between December and May) along the Amazon, the trees and bushes are sometimes completely submerged. There is as much as a 40-foot (12 m) drop in the height of the river between the dry season and the rainy season. Photo by Dr. Herbert R. Axelrod.

The fish that get trapped in these stagnant waters are crowded together. That a school of piranhas cut off in this way and faced with an increasing shortage of food becomes more aggressive and more dangerous to man and beast than it would be under normal circumstances is perfectly logical. Many a horse and ox has had chunks of flesh bitten out of their lips by piranhas at the watering place after unsuspectingly attempting to quench their thirst at a "lagoon" teeming with trapped, hungry piranhas. Reports about the "killer fish" should be subjected to closer scrutiny, with the phenomenon described here being kept in mind!

The water temperatures in tropical streams lie almost without exception between 26 and 30°C (79-86°F). The fluctuations occurring between day and night amount to less than one degree. The cycles of all chemical and biological matter and thus the vital processes of every aquatic organism from the algae to the fishes are intensified and accelerated by this unvarying heat. The constant high temperatures that govern all vital processes here can be compared to a permanently and fully depressed accelerator pedal of a car.

The great heat results in metabolic rates that are about four to five times as high as those in the rivers of central Europe. Grzimek has enlarged on this comparison by pointing out that, for example, the maturation of the eggs in tropical characins (family Characidae) only takes about 48 hours, whereas in the related minnows and daces (Cyprinidae) in European waters it takes six to eight days on an average. The high temperatures of the tropics further ensure that all nutrients that are liberated by processes of decomposition or that get into the water from the land are present either not at all or only very briefly, since the living organisms absorb and recycle them again immediately.

The tides of the Atlantic still make themselves felt in the Amazon as constantly rising and falling water levels, 800 kilometers (almost 500 miles) upstream. A phenomenon referred to as *amacunu* (water cloud noise) by the Indians is the natural feature of the Amazon that they are least able to comprehend: a tidal wave often more than 5 meters (16 feet) high that recurs at regular intervals. Twice a month, at new moon and full moon, the masses of water carried by this gigantic stream collide far out in the sea with the spring tide that is rolling landward at that time. The Amazon turns against itself with a roaring, mightly wall of water, the *pororoca*. Hoffmann in 1952 described the "great flood" as one of nature's wonders:

*Periodically the water reverses its direction when the At-
lantic flows in and drives the water of the Amazon before
it and pushes and shoves. Then the Amazon flows up to
700 kilometers (420 miles) inland. Suddenly the water
level rises and the floating islands, trees, and ships remain
motionless for a moment and are then rapidly swept away
in a westerly direction. The steamboats hurriedly seek
shelter in the mouth of the nearest tributary.*

*The masses of freshwater offer an increasing resistance
to the saltwater that is pressing against them. With growing
force they seek to hold their own—until the compressed
mass explodes. In a frightful clash the waters rise 6 to 8
meters (20-26 feet) above the high-water mark, forming a
wall. Thunderously they fall back, only to rise again and
thunderously sink once more, five to six times. This is what
is known as the* pororoca, *the flooding of the Amazon
plain by the sea. As soon as silence sets in, the land on
both sides of the river can be seen to have been flooded
for kilometers. Of the few people who live on these river-
banks, some have probably met their death, a small number of domestic animals have perished, a few houses have
been smashed or swept away, and here and there a boat
is hanging in the tops of a clump of trees. Soon the alluvial
land lies under the lead-gray cloud layer again out of
which, punctually, at their hour, the warm rains descend.*

As vividly as the great, cyclically recurring tidal wave has been
described here, one fact has not been mentioned. It is true that domestic animals are killed by it, and almost certainly some human
beings as well. However, the majority of flood victims in the millen-
nia during which the *pororoca* has been influencing the land by the
sides of this large river has always consisted of countless wild animals. The destructive masses of water seize them on the banks, in
treetops near the bank, and even on the ground in forests many kilometers away from the river.

If a catastrophe like the *pororoca* suddenly loads the already
highly active water with very many dead animals, the spread of
contagious diseases through these masses of decaying cadavers
would be phenomenal. But in this "great flood" that periodically
threatens the equilibrium of the tropical rivers in South America, the
piranhas in particular occupy the ecological niche of carrion-eaters
and are the only fast-acting health squad "assigned" the task of

cleaning up the waters. With great regularity, piranhas are found in the slow-flowing regions of the river, in "dead arms," and even in stagnant waters connected with the stream only from time to time.

Of course piranhas also attack living creatures, sometimes sick or injured ones or those that lack the capacity to survive. New tales

This is the Rio Abacaxis during the height of the rainy season when the waters of the Rio Madeira back up into this normally black-water river. Stones along the embankment are a rarity in the Amazonian area. Photo by Dr. Herbert R. Axelrod.

about this—variations on a theme—are only too frequent. Their other ecologically important function, however, tends to be largely ignored in these sensational reports. In their role as carrion-eaters, they clear the waters of any dead creatures long before they get a chance to putrefy in the warm water. It is this extremely important role played by piranhas in the ecosystem of the South American rivers and streams that has so far hardly been brought to the general public's attention with the necessary emphasis.

Piranhas may have evolved as efficient health squads, eating up the dead and dying that might otherwise pollute the waters. Drawn by Yuri Kaverkin.

A comparison with terrestrial utilizers of carrion is by no means far-fetched. Once you have arrived at that comparison, the bio-ecological function of piranhas certainly justifies the designation freshwater hyenas or freshwater vultures. Indeed, piranhas combine different modes of behavior typical of both terrestrial carrion-eaters. Like hyenas, piranhas sometimes hunt on their own or in small groups. Like them, they feed not only on carrion, but over and above that, attack everything that is injured, sick, weak, or unfit to live very long. Like the vultures, they often occur at the feeding place in large numbers and act as a health squad by utilizing everything except the skeleton.

If the piranhas evolved as an efficient health squad in the ecosystems of South American tropical rivers, why are they absent from the warm, humid tropics of Africa, for example? The basic prerequisites appear to be identical or similar there: a humid, warm, tropical climate (and consequently a bio-machinery that is running in high-gear). Like the Amazon, a gigantic stream (the Congo) forms an immense river system that flows through a basin where rain forests grow and pours into the sea at an average of 40,000 cubic meters of water per second (about 1,400,000 cubic feet).

The main difference from the South American basin landscape lies in the relief conditions. Whereas at a distance of 3500 kilometers (2000 miles) from the mouth the Amazon flows at an altitude of no more than 150 meters (500 feet) above sea level, the inner Congo basin lies at an average altitude of 400 meters (1300 feet). At that type of gradient, high water cannot have the same disastrous effects. What is absent is the "carrion producing" catastrophic flooding that has been making its cyclic appearance in South America for geological epochs. Hence the possible explanation for the absence of piranhas from tropical Africa is simply and logically this: the evolution of a specialized underwater health squad was totally unnecessary and did not take place.

Most of the piranhas to be found throughout the Amazon are the red-bellied kind, known scientifically as *Serrasalmus nattereri*. Most of them are about 6" (15 cm) in length. Photo by Heiko Bleher.

Keeping and Maintenance

Keeping fishes in captivity is a very old custom. The ancient Romans 2000 years ago kept fish in special tanks that were often designed to look like ponds. However, what motivated the fish keepers in antiquity was not so much the beautiful sight of the fish as the culinary delight in fresh fish. Contemporary Roman historians also describe some rather macabre "keeping practices" here and there. For example, to make the flesh of moray eels especially tender, they were fed on living slaves who were pushed into the eel tanks at regular intervals!

The keeping of fish in glass containers and aquaria primarily for esthetic reasons began in ancient China, where the goldfish was cultivated in grotesque forms. In Europe, aquaria have been in existence only since the beginning of the 19th century. Show-tanks in London and Paris, among the first of their kind to be on public display, also date back to the 19th century.

Today the keeping and observation of ornamental fishes has become a very popular hobby all over the world. In many areas, those who pursue it (aquarists) have organized themselves into clubs and societies, and special hobbyist magazines are being published as well.

There is an ever-increasing interest today in tropical ornamental fishes and their care. In the paragraphs that follow, the keeping and general maintenance of piranhas will be dealt with, since more recently they, too, have found their way into our home aquaria as scaly domestic animals. Meanwhile, the interest of private hobbyists in piranhas has grown so strong that some dealers actually have difficulties in getting enough supplies and are not always able to meet the demand.

As a rule, piranhas are offered on the market as silvery, black-speckled fry about the size of a quarter. The majority offered for sale are imported wild catches from the Orinoco and Amazon. The species *Serrasalmus nattereri* and *S. nigricans* come onto the market fairly frequently, but other species—such as *Serrasalmus rhombeus, Serrasalmus piraya,* etc.—are seldom available.

A complete ban on imports has been considered by some countries on a number of occasions. It was feared that the piranhas might be released from captivity and perhaps multiply in the wild, developing populations that had adapted to the changed environment. This fear turned out to be unfounded, however, since it would ap-

A fully matured *Serrasalmus nattereri* photographed in an aquarium.

pear that piranhas are able to reproduce only in very specific conditions.

My aquaria have been stocked with piranhas for many years. One thing this experience has taught me is that much of what is constantly being said about the keeping of these "dangerous aquatic beasts" can confidently be consigned to the realm of fable. The most important hints on keeping piranhas, as well as the necessary prerequisites, are summarized briefly below.

Tank Size

The newly bought piranhas must be offered an environment of adequate size. It is important, therefore, not to worry about cost where the size of the tank is concerned. Even if the fish measure no more than 2 to 4 centimeters (1-2 inches) at first, they grow exceedingly quickly. Any tank with a capacity of less than 100 liters (26 U.S. gallons) is unsuitable for keeping piranhas! The simple rule is: the bigger the tank, the better. Ample swimming space guarantees healthy, normal fish that under most favorable conditions even get down to spawning.

Water Conditions and Filtration

The water temperatures in the piranha tank should lie within the range of 24 to 27°C (75-81°F). An average temperature of 26°C (79°F) is best. The thermostats available on the market control the operation of the heater and ensure that the water temperature is more or less constant.

Where the water chemistry is concerned, piranhas seem to be amazingly tolerant. Although it is generally recommended that they should be kept in soft, slightly acid water with a total hardness of 5-10 DH and a pH of 6.5, fish kept at the Zurich Zoo actually spawned in much harder water (18-19 DH) as well, according to Honegger. Higher pH values are tolerated, even those above neutral (7) and up to around 8.5. Soft and slightly acid water more like that found in tropical conditions is produced, for example, by filtering over peat or by adding either peat extracts or tannic acid in liquid form. Your local pet shop should have these. The filtration should be carried out by means of efficient outside filters. Where the water enters by a jet that has been fitted above the surface, any additional aeration is generally superfluous.

Light Conditions

Piranhas are by nature very shy and nervous, and they take fright extremely readily. If the tank is exposed to glaring light, the characteristics just mentioned noticeably intensify. It is therefore advisable to keep the fish in fairly soft light conditions. This can be achieved, for instance, by using warm white fluorescent tubes, by covering the aquarium with a pane of frosted glass, or by cultivating a dense cover of floating plants. Pet shops usually sell warm white tubes.

Planting and Arranging the Tank

Although piranhas sometimes destroy water plants by chewing them, there is no reason for not having a well-planted (and in places densely planted) tank. There can be no doubt that dense vegetation actually and decisively contributes to the well-being of these ner-

High-powered filters such as the canister types are ideal for the piranha tank. Your local pet shop will propably have many types of power filters. Photo courtesy of Hagen.

vous creatures. Even fully grown fish constantly seek refuge in plant thickets when in danger.

Such plant thickets are best arranged along the back or one of the side walls of the tank so the fish can more readily be observed and fed in the front. Always make sure that there is adequate swimming space (about three-quarters of the tank). Suitable submersed plants include Java fern (*Microsorium pteropus*); the moss *Fontinalis; Echinodorus; Cryptocoryne; Aponogeton,* and *Vallisneria.* Depending on what light conditions prevail, the following are suitable as floating plants: duckweed (*Lemna minor*); *Azolla* sp.; and floating fern (*Salvinia natans*).

Bog roots and driftwood serve not only as decor, but offer additional hiding places. Before being put into the aquarium they should be thoroughly boiled, however. This ensures that any disease-producing organisms are destroyed. All the water absorbed by the roots usually makes additional weighting unnecessary. Only use roots obtained at your pet shop, as garden-quality roots may be poisonous!

Stocking the Tank With Fish

Only when all the necessary preparatory work has been completed can we begin to stock the aquarium with fish. Important, above all, is prior control of the water temperature or a check as to whether it remains constant at 25-26°C (78°F) as desired.

Planted aquaria will allow piranhas to exhibit natural behavior patterns. Photo by R. Stawikowski.

First of all, to avoid temperature shock the closed plastic bag with its newly acquired living contents must be hung inside the tank for 15 minutes to facilitate adjustment. Only then can the piranhas be released from the cramped confines of the bag in which they were packed. Be careful with bigger piranhas that can bite through plastic bags and aquarium nets without difficulty! They are more suitably transported in a large bucket with a tight-fitting lid. The water in this container should be enriched with oxygen by means of special tablets available for this purpose. Adequate heat insulation (as with newsprint) must also be provided in every case. Since older piranhas also destroy every net, I have for years been successfully using the perforated plastic insert of a bait bucket such as is available on the market for anglers.

Newly transferred piranhas tend to dart about aimlessly at first or escape into the nearest plant thicket. Young piranhas can also be observed to play dead—very convincingly—by lying down flat on the bottom. In some cases this type of behavior is continued even after the early stages of acclimation as soon as the keeper's hand is busy inside the tank. Within just a few hours, young *S. nattereri,* for example, begin to mark out territories fiercely defended against intruders. Even plant debris floating about in the water is attacked.

Just like older fish, young piranhas are well-versed in the repertoire of threat and submissive postures characteristic of the species. If, for instance, a quick movement of the hand in front of the tank makes the fish feel they are in danger, their initial reaction is to disperse frantically. Immediately afterward, however, they come together again to form a dense shoal at midwater depth. Obliquely, pointing slightly downward and with "drooping" tailfin and rapidly fanning pectoral fins, they stand within a centimeter (½ inch) of one another. At the same time, the whole axis of the body is slightly bent. This makes the posture of the young fish appear "contracted"—they look ready to shoot off in a frantic getaway at any moment.

It seems reasonable to assume that the same modes of behavior and "tricks" are also triggered or applied in nature when danger threatens (for instance, when a natural enemy is encountered), since they would be extremely effective in those circumstances, too. Predacious fishes virtually always are helpless when confronted with a dense shoal of potential food fish—they need to be able to concentrate on individual prey. In a dense shoal with identical movements, they fail, so to speak, to see the forest for the trees. This overwhelming stimulation can unnerve a predator so much that no attack takes place. To larger predators a young piranha is just another foodfish. Once it has been expelled from the security of the shoal, there is only one thing left for the young fish: frantic flight. If cornered, the fish plays dead.

Closer contact with the shoal is not entirely without its problems for the young piranhas, however. If under normal conditions closer contact results in threatening behavior or a mock attack, it is entirely logical that this often happens in an accentuated way when

Regular partial changes of the water in an aquarium are of great benefit to the fishes. Such changes can be made with siphons and buckets or in a labor-saving manner through the use of water-changing equiptment available in pet shops. Photo courtesy of Aquarium Products.

Products for treating the aquarium's water to make it safer for the fish to live in are available at pet shops. Some also put a protective coating on the fish and detoxify certain highly poisonous metallic salts. Photo courtesy of Aquarium Pharmaceuticals.

the fish are in a state of excitement (such as stress caused by fear). After the situation has calmed down, you can see a sudden change in behavior. Every fish quickly distances itself from its neighbor and the tight shoal breaks up. At once the old territories beneath roots and the overhanging leaves of aquatic plants are occupied again.

While clearly seeking refuge in a dense shoal (driven together by fear) when threatened with danger, the fish appear to prefer a greater distance—a distance from members of the same species that guarantees personal safety—the rest of the time.

During the first few weeks and months, the best time to observe the fish is in the evenings. Then movements outside the tank go un-noticed by them and they lose their shyness.

Feeding

Basically, young piranhas snap at anything that floats about in the water and is the size of a morsel of food. Apart from dried food, the fish should be given live food in the form of tubificid worms and bloodworms or frozen beef heart during the first weeks and months of acclimation. Pet shops sell many live foods. Escaped tubificid worms that come wriggling out of the bottom at a later date are first eyed from an oblique position and then, having thus been "sized up," are furiously pulled out. Mosquito larvae quivering about in the open water are overpowered by wild, jerking forward thrusts that seem to follow from the normal swimming movements without a break. When young piranhas are feeding, they often shoot up to the surface of the water to snap at mosquito larvae floating there. When swallowing the wriggling prey, the fry generally make violent shaking movements.

Piranhas are easily conditioned to approach the feeding spot when they see their "master" approaching. This group of piranhas approached the photographer no matter where he positioned himself. Photo of *Serrasalmus nattereri* by Dr. Herbert R. Axelrod.

The same shaking movements can be observed when the first morsels of fish and meat are accepted. Because of their nutritional value and vitamin content, heart and liver are particularly suitable as foods. To prevent calcium deficiency, the piranhas should also be supplied with foodfishes as often as possible. Pet shops sell feeder goldfish for this purpose. The fish or pieces of meat (earthworms also are accepted) can simply be thrown in at a certain spot or can be tied to a thread and lowered into the tank. The thread method has the advantage of always enabling you to offer the food in the optimum position (about 5 to 6 centimeters, 2-2½", above the bottom) in exactly the same place.

As soon as the morsel of food has been spotted, all the fish begin to "lie in wait" for it. Soon the first fish comes shooting forward, and then everything happens at lightning speed. No detour is made to attack the "prey." The young piranha sinks its teeth into it and carries out rapid, violent shaking movements with the body. The darting forth, sinking in of the teeth, shaking, and removal of a bite take only seconds. All that remains is a clean hemispherical hole in the piece of food.

Flake foods, available in a variety of conveniently sized packages, are among the most commonly offered fish food. Photo courtesy of Wardley.

Piranhas, like sharks, are apprehensive feeders in unknown situations. As soon as one fish starts to feed, however, the others join in, sort of in a feeding frenzy. Drawn by Yuri Kaverkin.

The rushing forward to feed by the first fish generally acts as a signal for all the others. They, too, dart out of hiding immediately and collect their share. At this moment not even the light from several powerful electronic flashes used in photographing the feeding process can do anything to frighten them, shy though they are at other times.

During this initial greedy feeding, two or three fish sometimes sink their teeth into the food at once and pull it to and fro with their wild shaking movements. Minor squabbles among the fish are very common, and after feeding one or another of the piranhas swims about with fins that have neat hemispherical pieces missing. These harmless wounds usually heal within a week.

When feeding is over, there is a clearly noticeable digestive phase. This is characterized by increased passivity. Every fish moves into its favorite place and stands there quite calmly, usually at an appropriate distance from the other members of the species. At this time the head is always pointed toward that part of the aquarium where the aerated water flows into the tank after having passed through the outside filter. If one changes the location from which the water flows in, the fish invariably adjust their positions accordingly. The piranhas thus adopt a position in which their bodies offer the least resistance to the water and in which they can let the oxygen, of which an increased amount is needed to facilitate digestion, flow through the gills to their best advantage.

From time to time squabbles break out among older fish in captivity. Here the biting is more serious, however. During feeding in a state of extreme excitement, it can even happen that an individual fish of the same species has pieces of flesh torn out of its back or flanks. As a rule, even deep wounds heal up amazingly quickly, however. Piranhas enjoy an impressive capacity for regeneration. Cannibalism does occur, however. In smaller tanks it is not uncommon that of a whole shoal of fry originally put in, only one or two strong specimens remain to grow into adults.

The staple diet of large piranhas should consist of rather large pieces of heart, liver, and muscle, and, above all, of live fish. The piranhas may be given smaller portions of food every day or larger portions every other day. Sometimes adult piranhas go through regular fasting periods on their own accord. They also leave the food untouched if there are any unusual disturbances prior to feeding.

Earthworms remain very popular with adult piranhas, too, and are frequently caught before they have reached the bottom of the aquarium. On the bottom the worms go on crawling, even under water, and consequently are picked up much more quickly than, for example, a piece of meat that lies motionless at the bottom. Smaller

A school of *Serrasalmus nattereri*. They stay in a loose school waiting to be fed. Photo by Jorg Vierke.

worms immediately are swallowed whole. Larger and more lively worms are also picked up whole, but immediately afterward the piranha retreats into a quiet corner of the tank where it spits out the worm a few times and swallows it again. Each time the worm passes through the shredder formed by the rows of sharp teeth. This process is repeated until the worm has stopped moving and has been chopped into pieces. All this happens very quickly, since the fish has to be prepared for the eventuality of being robbed of its prey by an envious member of its own species when it spits out the worm.

An observation made at Duisburg Zoo proves that the color red acts as a trigger for an attack. A few goldfish and Crucian carp had been put into the tank as foodfishes. Whereas the dark brownish wild Crucian carp were given comparatively little attention at first, the conspicuous goldfish were consistently chased by several piranhas. Another unusual fact is that even fully grown piranhas still eat daphnia (water fleas), as I have observed repeatedly.

Old food remnants must be removed at regular intervals. The "mulm corner" of the tank should also be cleaned once a week with a siphon. My piranhas have never suffered from fungal diseases, but you should beware of confusing aggressive behavior with immunity to dirt and diseases. Cleanliness and hygiene must receive top priority in an environment bounded by glass walls, and they can be improved decisively by administering the food in correct quantities!

Fiction and Fact

In numerous publications, both past and present, you may read that piranhas can only be kept on their own or in single-species tanks with other piranhas. This actually is not true. Piranhas can be kept in association with armored catfishes and bristlenoses without any problems, and sometimes even with small guppies or small species of characins. The occasional minor accident can happen, of course, but if fed adequately, piranhas tolerate a few other occupants. Only fishes that are reeling about or are obviously sick are promptly attacked. Bristlenoses (*Ancistrus multispinus,* etc.) are especially suitable for the pirana aquarium because of the unappetizing spines on their bodies and their zealous removal of algae. For precisely these reasons bristlenoses are being kept in association with piranhas in numerous public aquaria.

The red-tailed black shark (*Labeo bicolor*) also can usually be kept in association with immature piranhas without difficulty. This is another species that browses on algae and is intelligent enough

quickly to dive for the nearest cover when things get tricky. Sometimes a young red-tailed black shark actually attaches itself to a
shoal of young piranhas and moves through the tank with them.

For a time I kept a small shoal of *Serrasalmus nigricans* about 12
cm (5 inches) in length together with a vegetarian metynnis (*Metynnis rooseveltiella*). The latter was tolerated in the group and was
never attacked. Since the species *M. rooseveltiella* bears a strong
general resemblance to its dangerous cousins, the biting instinct is
effectively inhibited. It is, therefore, perfectly possible as a rule to
keep piranhas and *M. rooseveltiella* in the same tank, provided the
fish are identical in size.

I would also like to point out here that, contrary to all reports that
say otherwise, numerous essential tasks in the tank can be carried
out perfectly safely with bare hands. As soon as the keeper's hand
is plunged into the water, most piranhas will take fright and vanish
into plant thickets. Of course, you should make sure that the fish are
well-fed and that your hands are free from bleeding wounds. Furthermore, all movements must be made as slowly and calmly as
possible so that no panic breaks out among the fish. Only panic or
the feeling of being cornered is likely to provoke an attack. If some-
one is going to stick loose bushes of water plants into the bottom
with his bare hands when a fully grown, very frightened piranha has
just hidden itself among them, then he has only himself to blame if
he is left with four fingers on one hand. On second thought, perhaps
it would just be safer not to put your hands into any piranha tank.

Piranhas in Public Aquaria

Serrasalmus species are now on view in most zoos and public
aquaria. For many an average aquarium their presence ensures that
the number of visitors remains at a secure level, and it is under-
standable that those in authority at the zoos are aware of this effect,
too.

The following are details of the conditions in which piranhas are
at present being kept in the show tanks of a variety of German zoological gardens and aquaria. Particular attention has been paid to
the water temperature, the water chemistry (pH value, water hardness), and diet.

BERLIN (West) • Aquarium/Terrarium
Species: *Serrasalmus nattereri.* **Tank size:** c. 400 liters (100 U.S. gallons). **Water:** temperature c. 26°C (79°F). **Diet:** fish meat (e.g., pink
salmon).

BOCHUM • Zoo
Species: *Serrasalmus nattereri.* **Tank size:** c. 600 liters (150 U.S. gallons). **Water:** temperature c. 25°C (77°F), pH 7, hardness 11 DH.

PUBLIC AQUARIUM SPECIAL
Watch the piranhas as
they eat, swim, breed, fight and kill.
ADULTS ONLY...no kids.

Diet: dead chicks, fish twice weekly. The dried food thrown in every day for a few bristlenoses also is eaten by the piranhas.

DUISBURG • Aquarium in the Zoological Gardens
Species: *Serrasalmus nattereri.* **Tank size:** c. 4500 liters (1200 U.S. gallons). **Water:** temperature 20-25°C (68-77°F). **Diet:** meat, live fish (Crucian carp, goldfish, etc.).

DUESSELDORF • Loebbecke Museum and Aquarium
Species: *Serrasalmus nattereri.* **Tank size:** c. 1000 liters (260 U.S. gallons). **Water:** temperature c. 26°C (77°F), extra soft (ion exchanger), filtered over Ehfi substrate (coarse) and granulated lava material. **Diet:** muscle meat, ox heart, filleted fish, krill (deep-frozen) every other day.

ESSEN • Aquarium in the Gruga
Species: *Serrasalmus aureus* (more likely = *S. nigricans*). **Tank size:** c. 1800 liters (500 U.S. gallons). **Water:** temperature 25°C (77°F) slightly acid. **Diet:** every other day, filleted fish (salmon or Norway haddock) and squashed Crucian carps given alternately.

FRANKFURT ● Aquarium in the Zoological Gardens
Species: probably *Serrasalmus piraya.* **Tank size:** c. 3500 liters (900 U.S. gallons). **Water:** temperature 24°C (75°F), pH 7, hardness 12 DH. **Diet:** fed once to twice a week.

HAMBURG ● Aquarium in the Hagenbeck Zoological Gardens
Species: *Serrasalmus nattereri* (bred in captivity in Zurich). **Tank size:** c. 500 liters (130 U.S. gallons). **Water:** temperature 25°C (77°F), hardness 12 DH, very high oxygen content. **Diet:** freshwater fishes.

COLOGNE ● Aquarium at the Zoo
Species: *Serrasalmus nattereri* (at present about 150 specimens originating from Zurich). **Tank size:** c. 15,000 liters (4000 U.S. gallons), with "rain-forest panorama." **Water:** temperature 25°C (77°F), pH 6.2, hardness 8 DH, carbonate hardness 1 CH, cleaning is carried out by means of a multiple-stage filter with a total area of 4 m² (4.8 sq. yds.), 10 m³ (350 cubic feet) of water circulated per hour. **Diet:** meat, fish meat.

MANNHEIM ● Aquarium in the Luisenpark
Species: possibly *Serrasalmus nigricans.* **Tank size:** c. 1500 liters (400 U.S. gallons). **Water:** temperature 25-26°C (77°F). **Diet:** fish meat.

MUNICH ● Aquarium in the Zoological Gardens Hellabrunn
Species: possibly *Serrasalmus piraya.* **Tank size:** 10,000 liters (2500 U.S. gallons). **Water:** temperature 24-26°C (75-79 F). **Feeding:** twice weekly, raw horse heart cut into small pieces, horse meat, whitefish from time to time.

MUENSTER ● Aquarium in the Allwetter Zoo
Species: *Serrasalmus nattereri.* **Tank size: c. 1045 liters (275 U.S. gallons). Water:** temperature c. 25°C (77°F), hardness 7.8 DH, filtration over Ehfi substrate (coarse). **Diet:** ox heart and dried food in tablet form every other day.

STUTTGART ● Aquarium in the Wilhelma
Species: *Serrasalmus nattereri.* **Tank size:** no information. **Water:** temperature c. 25°C (77°F) (raised to c. 28°C during the spawning season in April/May), hardness 5-10 DH, pH 7-8. **Diet:** freshwater fishes, lean heart and muscle meat (in small quantities) at regular intervals.

Breeding

Piranhas are among those species of fishes that do not often reproduce in captivity, and breeding is difficult and exceptional. Specific literature is extremely scant and at the present time is confined to just a few breeding reports.

The following basic requirements must be satisfied for successful spawning:
1) a small shoal of piranhas that are sexually mature or ready to spawn; 2) a species tank of 1000 liters (250 U.S. gallons) minimum, provided with hiding places and containing water plants; 3) a water temperature that has been raised to 28-30°C (82-86°F).

What appears to have been the first successful attempt at breeding piranhas in captivity, in the U.S.A., dates back to 1960. It was William Braker, at the John G. Shedd Aquarium in Chicago, who got piranhas of the less dangerous species *Serrasalmus spilopleura* (Kner) to reproduce themselves. The fish had been living in an aquarium of about 4500 liters (1200 U.S. gallons) capacity for three

There is no great mystery about spawning piranhas, or any other fish for that matter. The same procedure must be followed. You must have at least a male and female in breeding condition. They must be fully acclimated to their aquarium, and the aquarium must be very large and have suitable "nesting" facilities. Feeding living foods, especially "feeder" goldfish, is a necessity. Drawn by Yuri Kaverkin.

years and at the time of spawning had a body length of about 18 cm (7 inches). The female very carefully laid the eggs on water plants, and afterward the spawn was guarded by the male. The latter also protected the brood, which hatched after five days.

In Germany, piranhas were first bred in captivity with success in 1963. This was at Duisburg Zoo, and the species involved was *Serrasalmus rhombeus* (L.). What follows relates to the breeding report by Gedaschke as presented in 1969, with additional information by Dr. Gewalt, the Director of the Zoo.

The piranhas, originally classified as *Serrasalmus niger,* had been obtained from Holland in 1955 as fry measuring 2.5-3.5 centimeters (1-1½ inches) in length. After acclimation they were transferred to a display tank of about 4500 liters (1200 U.S. gallons) capacity. Roots served as hiding places, and in addition, the tank had been densely planted with *Cryptocoryne* species, *Echinodorus, Aponogeton,* and *Vallisneria.* Through cannibalism, the piranhas—a total of 20 initially—eventually reduced themselves to six specimens. By 1963, after having been kept for eight years, they had attained a length of 26-32 centimeters (10-13 inches) and a height of 12-20 centimeters (5-8 inches). The fish had spawned on several occasions, but without any young developing. Each time, the eggs that were removed grew mycotic (covered with fungus).

On the evening of 20 August, 1963, eggs were shed again from 1900 to 2000 hours. The spawn (about 1500 to 1600 eggs) was deposited in dense moss near the root of a tree on this occasion. Although fiercely defended by the parent animals, half the eggs that had been laid were successfully siphoned off. These were distributed over four all-glass tanks that had been prepared for this eventuality. To ensure that the spawning temperature was exactly maintained, the all-glass tanks, which had been specially aerated, were hung inside the display tank. They contained:

Tank 1: Display tank water with methylene blue;
Tank 2: Display tank water with methylene blue and 50% distilled water;
Tank 3: 95% distilled water, 5% tank water and Cilex breeding aid;
Tank 4: Display tank water only.
The sequence of development was as follows:
21 August: Roughly the same quantity of eggs in all four tanks had grown mycotic; the mycotic eggs were removed with a pipette.
22 August: At about 1300 hours, the first embryonic movements within the eggs could be seen in Tank 4. Hatching soon occurred. At about 1530 hours, ditto in the other tanks. This evening all living embryos or fry were taken out with a pipette and put into an all-glass tank containing 95% distilled water, 5% tank water, and Cilex breeding aid.

Two *Serrasalmus nattereri* spawning. They spawn like most characins, rubbing their bodies together as they release sperm and eggs, except that they spawn in a pre-conditioned nest and deposit their spawn on the nest as shown here. Photo by Hiroshi Azuma.

23 August: All living fry—about 750—were transferred to a tank without Cilex. Water temperature was kept constant at 25°C (77°F). The water was crystal-clear, filtration with a PS flat filter over glass wool and charcoal.

25 August: Eyes clearly discernible; jerky, reeling movements; body length about 7-8 mm (¼-⅓ inch).

27 August: Temperature was raised to nearly 28°C (82°F) and the aeration increased. The fry stood facing the current. Yolk sac still clearly visible.

28 August: Moss (*Fontinalis*) was put into the tank and individual fry attached themselves to it. Toward 2300 hours all the fry swam free.

29 August: The majority of the fry were still hanging in the moss. At around 1830 hours the first feeding attempts were made with brine shrimp. At around 2000 hours all the young were lying at the bottom. At around 2200 hours they were swimming about in the dark in a lively manner.

Tropical Fish Hobbyist magazine, July, 1975, published the first color-illustrated article on the spawning of a piranha. It was written by Hiroshi Azuma, a Japanese specialist in breeding very rare fishes. His photographs show the piranha pair making a nest as shown below.

As soon as the nest is completed, the pair start spawning. They line their bodies up and shed sperm and eggs onto the selected spawning site. Azuma used small rocks to hold the coconut fiber spawning grass in position. Photo by Hiroshi Azuma.

30 August: 50-60 fry were swimming about, and the rest were lying at the bottom. It was not possible to tell if they were still resorbing the yolk sac or had already fed actively. At around 2200, in the darkness, they were very lively; after the light had been switched on they lay motionless in a corner. Feeding on cyclops and small daphnia occurred at around 2300 hours.

31 August: At around 1400 and 2145 hours the fry were offered small daphnia again and these were undoubtedly swallowed.

1 September–8 September: The fry attained a length of about 10-12 mm (½ inch).

15 September: The fry were transferred to a tank of 50 x 35 cm (20 x 14 inches) and counted. They totaled 655 and measured anywhere between 15 and 20 mm (3/5-4/5 inch) in size.

On October 1, 1964, the young piranhas were over a year old and had developed very well. Twenty of them were put into the display tank with the adult fish, which caused no problems, the older fish and the young ones swimming peacefully side by side. The adult fish spawned again in 1964 and 1965. The spawn, which was left in the tank, was devoured, however. From 1966 on, the group of young fish, measuring about 15 cm (6 inches) in length at this stage had diminished in number considerably due to cannibalism, mainly attacks by the older fish. The exact number was difficult to establish since they kept to themselves carefully hidden among an unusually dense thicket of *Cryptocoryne* in the display tank.

There is literature available now on the breeding of *Serrasalmus nattereri* (Kner 1859). To date this has been accomplished at the Cincinnati Zoo, at the Zoological Gardens of Zurich, in the Aquaria of Cologne, and at the Duisburg Zoo, as well as (repeatedly) at the Stuttgart Wilhelma. The most detailed breeding report was that of Honegger in 1971, extensive passages from it being used below.

Since 1956, *Serrasalmus nattereri* (Kner 1859) (synonym: *Rooseveltiella nattereri*) have been kept at the Aquarium of Zurich Zoo in a tank of 100 x 70 x 60 cm (40 x 28 x 24 inches) planted with Java moss. The adult fish are fed on fresh, lean beef as well as fish meat given three times a week.

On 24 April 1970, the aquarium keeper, E. Christen, discovered a fairly large number of freshly laid eggs in the moss. The water temperature was 26°C (79°F) at the time. Since it was impossible to siphon off the spawn, the eggs were taken out of the aquarium complete with Java moss adhering to them. The male that had been guarding the eggs hid in the Java moss while this was going on. To minimize the risk at the time of hatching, some of the eggs were entrusted to an experienced breeder for maturation. The rest stayed at the Zoo.

The young hatched after four days. During the first few days they hung suspended from the moss, but later they lay distributed all over the bottom of the aquarium.

At the age of four days, they began to eat the smallest of brine shrimp. At a later stage they were given large quantities of copepods and water fleas. After no more than a few days, we were already able to observe how the young bit one another in the fins. Growth was rapid. At the age of two months, the biggest fry had attained a length of 45 mm (1-4/5 inches) and were attractively speckled. This juvenile coloration is lost with increasing age, however, the parent animals being steel-gray to steel-blue in color. At the end of December, 1970, when aged eight months, the largest fish were 120 mm (5 inches) long.

On 30 May, the adult fish spawned once more; some of the adult fish were badly bitten after spawning. The fish spawned for the third time on 22 September 1970, and this time, too, a few of the parent animals sustained severe injuries. Toward the evening of 24 December 1970, I observed how a male defended a certain spot in the aquarium against members of the same species. On the morning of 26 December, keeper E. Christen discovered fresh spawn in that spot. The male that was guarding the eggs was injured mainly on the head as well as on the flanks. Despite this defense, two-thirds of the eggs were devoured within 36 hours. The fry that had hatched from the remaining eggs gathered inside the filter basin over the next few days and from there were transferred to a separate raising tank.

So far none of the keepers have ever been injured by any of the adult piranhas in their care. As soon as any work is being carried out inside the tank, the fish retreat to the bottom and into their hiding places. Even when they are fed they withdraw at first. Remarks in the literature that adjustments inside the tank are only possible with the aid of sticks cannot be said to apply in all cases.

There are widely differing opinions, both in theory and practice, as to the water quality where the keeping and breeding of piranhas are concerned. Paysan in 1970 recommended that *Rooseveltiella nattereri* (= *S. nattereri*) be kept in soft water, 10° total hardness, with an addition of peat. The Zurich fish, on the other hand, are kept in fairly hard water of 18-19° total hardness.

In 1970 Géry suggested that, like the higher fishes, piranhas might practice brood care. That this assumption is correct has been confirmed by the Zurich observation.

According to a report by Jes in 1973, three specimens of *Serrasalmus nattereri* bred in Zurich arrived at the Aquarium of Cologne Zoo on 14 July 1970. After having been kept provisionally in two 400 liter (100 U.S. gallons) tanks they were transferred to the impressive 15,000 liter (3900 U.S. gallons) tank with a tropical river panorama. The water at that time had the following properties: a pH of 6.2, a total hardness of 6.7°, and a carbonate hardness of 2.5°. The piranhas measured between 9 and 12 centimeters (3½-5 inches) at this stage.

The actual breeding success in Cologne, however, was literally the result of an accident inside the display tank. Owing to there being a glass roof above the river landscape that allowed plenty of light to get in, the water grew very turbid from time to time due to a bloom of floating algae in the course of the first summer. Late in the summer, when the water had cleared, a hundred or so young piranhas about 2 to 4 centimeters (1-2 inches) long were noticed with great surprise. The removal of the brood turned out to be ex-

ceedingly difficult and was undertaken with the aid of a hand net,
a flat net, and at a later stage even by angling using a fine hook and
a steel leader. Because of the algal bloom that prevailed at the time
of spawning, it was not possible to make any observations regarding

Serrasalmus rhombeus as photographed by Dr. Herbert R. Axelrod. **Facing
page:** *Serrasalmus calmoni* in an aquarium setting.

the spawning process and brood care. A future "accident" of this
nature was prevented by means of UV lamps, but unfortunately this
measure also has prevented any further breeding success.

Numerous public aquaria have been supplied with young *S. nattereri* bred at the Stuttgart Wilhelma. The wild *S. nattereri* kept there
first spawned in May, 1974. Prior to spawning, the water temperature is always raised to about 28°C (82°F). Depending on the temperature, the young hatch after two to four days. The raising food
consists of nauplii of *Artemia* and cyclops. The total number of fry
raised always lies somewhere between 500 and 1000 specimens.
Adult males have repeatedly been observed to practice brood care.
So far no specific information has been published about piranha
culture in Stuttgart, and what I have written here was imparted to
me by Herr Podloucky, Stuttgart Wilhelma, in response to my
inquiry.

The fact that piranhas actually look after their brood is quite unusual for a characin. Before, during, and after spawning, the fishes'heightened aggressiveness results in increased biting attacks among themselves.

The water plants are often bitten off just above their bases, and the resultant bare patches are fiercely defended against members of the same species. Spawning usually takes place by night. A portion of the spawn is glued to what remains of the stalks of the water plants.

Ulrich, an employee at Duisburg Zoo, made detailed observations concerning the raising of the fry that hatched after about four days and fed on the microinfusorians that had been siphoned off from the display tank together with the brood. An analysis of the water resulted in the following astonishing data: total hardness 20°, carbonate hardness 9.0°, pH 7.3, nitrite 0.1, temperature 29.0°C (84°F). That the fish spawned in spite of such hard water is amazing, considering that their home rivers carry extremely soft water as a rule. When transferred to a 600 liter (150 U.S. gallons) tank, the fry developed quickly. Subsequently some of them were put back into the large display tank containing the parent fish. The fish are fed on live trout here, spectacular business from the visitor's point of view!

Taxonomic Survey

The work *Systema Naturae,* published by Linnaeus in 1758, constitutes what is the generally accepted starting point of a classification by scientific names formed by a combination of Latinized generic and specific names. Within this system of zoological classification, every species that lived or lives on earth occupies a fixed place and is given a scientific name. Following research by Darwin and others, the "artificial" system by Linnaeus, based more on external similarities, was to some extent replaced by a "natural" system that relied more strongly on relationships. Thanks to the ongoing, ever more detailed examination of the species, the systematic elements of zoological classification are constantly being improved and altered. This certainly applies to the systematics of fishes, the characins being a case in point.

The French ichthyologist Géry in 1970-72 published a new system classification of the characins. Instead of just the previous order Ostariophysi (=fishes with a bony connection between the air bladder and the labyrinth), Géry differentiated between two orders: catfish-like fishes (Siluriformes) and carp-like fishes (Cypriniformes). The latter were further divided into three suborders: 1) characins (Characoidei); 2) electric eels and knife-fishes (Gymnotoidei); and 3) carps (Cyprinoidei). Within this new system the characins (Characoidei) were categorized into 14 families, the second of which contains *Serrasalmus* (Serrasalmidae). The subfamily of Serrasalminae consists solely of the genus of true piranhas (*Serrasalmus* Lacépède, 1803) which is divided into four subgenera.

It must be pointed out here that as far as a satisfactory classification of the piranhas is concerned, taxonomy is still unsettled. Some "species" owe their recognition purely to the description of one or a few specimens. Where these fish were described rather superficially (based merely on body shape and coloration, which in the majority of piranhas are subject to constant change, depending on their developmental stage), the species has to be treated with a certain amount of caution.

The number of *Serrasalmus* species, as well as their subspecies, existing today is estimated by Géry (but opinions vary considerably in this respect) to come to more than 20. The systematics suggested below constitutes in effect a conglomeration compiled from the attempts at classification by other authors as well as my own observations and research in South America.

In Manaus, Brazil, at the INPA (roughly translated this stands for the National Institute for the Protection of the Amazon) laboratory, Dr. Axelrod instructs the faculty and students on fish photography. From left to right: Dr. Junk, Director of INPA, Dr. Bert Frank, Dr. Jacques Gery, and Dr. Herbert R. Axelrod.

Characoids of the World, by Dr. Jacques Gery, is the most complete and up-to-date work on the subject of piranhas and other characins. This book is available at most pet shops that carry aquarium fishes.

CLASSIFICATION OF PIRANHAS
Class: OSTEICHTHYES, bony fishes
Superorder: TELEOSTEI, true bony fishes
Order: CYPRINIFORMES, carp-like fishes
Suborder: CHARACOIDEI, characins
Family: SERRASALMIDAE, including *Serrasalmus*
Subfamily: SERRASALMINAE, piranha-like fishes
Genus: *SERRASALMUS,* piranhas, 4 subgenera and over 20 species.

I. Subgenus *Pygopristis*

This subgenus would seem to be the one that is the least specialized and the most difficult to delineate. Guianas region and perhaps
lower Amazon. Only one species (*S. denticulatus*) has so far been
described in detail. The existence and status of other described species (e.g., *Pygopristis antoni* from the Rio San José, Estado Guarico,
Venezuela) appears uncertain.

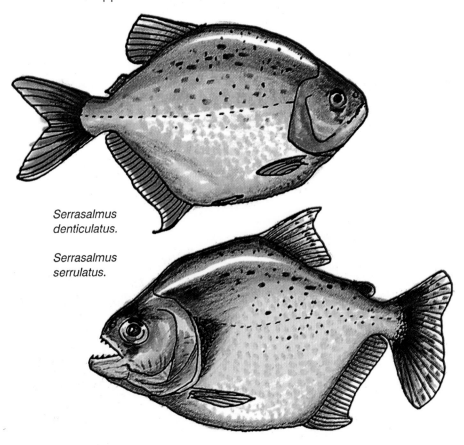

*Serrasalmus
denticulatus.*

*Serrasalmus
serrulatus.*

II. Subgenus *Pristobrycon*

The species of piranhas included in this subgenus are comparatively rare and appear to be less aggressive. Found in the lower and middle courses of the Amazon, the Guyana region, and the Orinoco delta. Nine species commonly are listed for the subgenus, but only two are distinctive; the other names probably are synonyms.

Serrasalmus aureus

Range: Brazil and possibly Caquiare-Orinoco region, Venezuela.

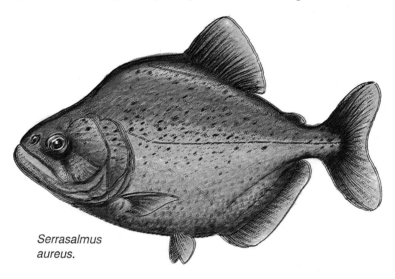

Serrasalmus aureus.

Serrasalmus emarginatus

Range: Possibly Surinam.

Serrasalmus serrulatus

Range: Amazon, Rio Atacavi (Venezuela).

A very large species attaining a length of 35-40 cm (14-16 inches). The specimen examined came from the Universidad Central Caracas. According to Mago-Leccia, this was the biggest *Serrasalmus* that had been caught in Venezuela so far.

Serrasalmus scapularis

Range: Rio Essequibo (Guyana).

Serrasalmus gymnogenys

Range: Surinam and lower course of the Amazon.

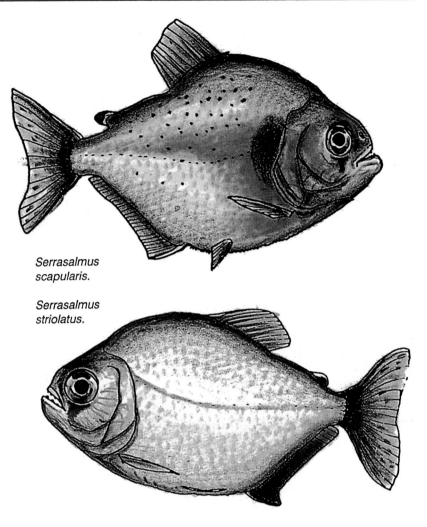

*Serrasalmus
scapularis.*

*Serrasalmus
striolatus.*

Serrasalmus striolatus
Range: Rio Para, Rio Tapanohony (Guyana region).

Serrasalmus calmoni
Range: Rio Para (Guyana).

Serrasalmus bilineatus
Range: Rio Aruca (Guyana region).

Serrasalmus coccogenis
Range: Venezuela.

III. Subgenus *Serrasalmus*

This subgenus comprises some four to six species and enjoys a very wide range of distribution. Members of this subgenus usually have a concave outline to the head and body.

Serrasalmus eigenmanni
Range: Rio Essequibo, Rio Potaro (Guyana region).

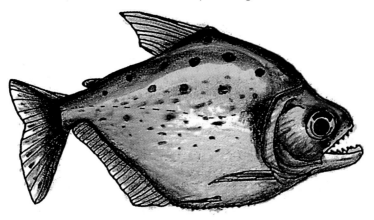

Serrasalmus eigenmanni.

Serrasalmus rhombeus
Range: Amazon and Orinoco regions and entire Guyana region.

There are 37-38 teeth on the ventral keel. Reaches a maximum length of 38 cm (17-18 inches). An aggressive species, widely distributed. Juvenile fish show silvery speckles and the fins are light in color and transparent like glass. Adult specimens grow very dark, in some cases completely black, and the shape of the body also alters. The body is strongly compressed laterally, and the snout shows a deep cleft. In profile the head is markedly concave. The palatine bones are covered with a total of 14 small teeth.

Serrasalmus hollandi
Distribution: Not known for certain.

A high-backed, compressed species. The back and head are dark gray to olive-green in color, while the upper half of the body looks dirty white to silvery and shows a few dark spots. Often there is a dark spot on the shoulder. The fins of immature animals are light, transparent. Old animals become almost totally black. This may be a subspecies or synonym of *S. rhombeus*.

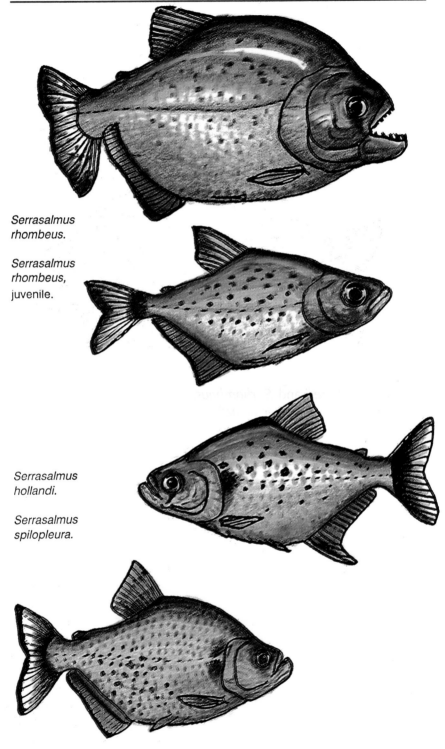

Serrasalmus
rhombeus.

Serrasalmus
rhombeus,
juvenile.

Serrasalmus
hollandi.

Serrasalmus
spilopleura.

Serrasalmus spilopleura

Distribution: Amazon as far as the La Plata plain, Orinoco region, Lago del Guarico (Venezuela).

29-36 teeth on the ventral keel. Maximum length about 25-30 cm (10-12 inches). A high-backed and very strongly compressed species. Immatures are silvery with numerous black speckles. With increasing age changes into a dirty indistinctly spotted gray fish. The head looks distinctly concave in profile. Red eyes. A total of ten small palatine teeth. Mouth deeply incised, the lower jaw conspicuously long and powerful with numerous teeth.

Serrasalmus niger

Distribution: Guianas.

The body is stocky and high-backed, laterally very strongly compressed. Maximum length about 35 cm (14 inches). In juveniles the body is likely to be light in color, with light, glassy fins. The characteristic blackish gray color of the body and fins does not appear until the fish are old. *S. niger* is an extremely aggressive species of piranha that is generally feared where it occurs. In the aquarium, the black piranha is said to attack anything that moves.

Many piranhas whose color had darkened with age were erroneously classifed as *S. niger* by various authors, especially adult specimens of *S. nattereri* and *S. rhombeus*.

That the species *S. niger* actually exists is not yet regarded as an absolute certainty.

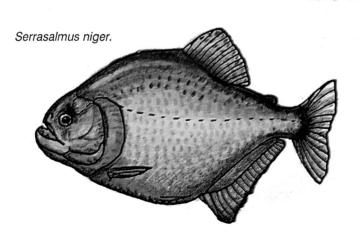

Serrasalmus niger.

IV. Subgenus *Taddyella*

There are probably no more than four to five species, some of which look very much alike. As opposed to the subgenus *Serrasalmus,* members of the subgenus *Taddyella* are characterized by showing a convex outline of the head and body.

Serrasalmus piraya

Distribution: Lower Amazon region, Rio Sao Francisco (Brazil).

22-24 teeth along the ventral keel. Maximum length about 50 cm (20 inches), so likely to be the largest species of piranha. The body is extremely stocky and laterally compressed. The head is comparatively large, the domed forehead high. Basic coloration of back and flanks is olive-brown, laterally very iridescent. The lower regions of the body are more orange-red in color. Adult specimens are difficult to distinguish from *S. nattereri,* except that they possess a tufted, fibrous adipose fin.

Serrasalmus nattereri

Distribution: Beyond a doubt the most widely distributed species: Amazon and Orinoco region, all Guianan countries, as well as the

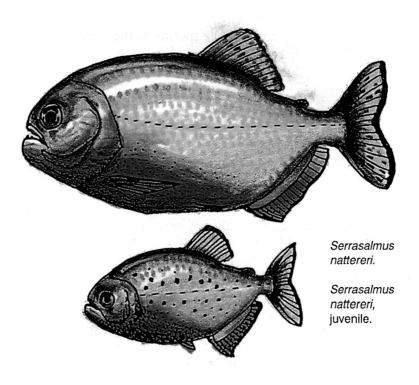

Serrasalmus nattereri.

Serrasalmus nattereri, juvenile.

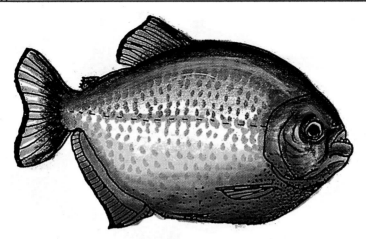

Serrasalmus piraya. The German word for piranha is *piraya.*

Rio Paraguay and Rio Parana.

28-31 teeth along the ventral keel. The body is stocky and later-ally compressed, maximum length 30-32 cm (12-13 inches). The caudal fin is only slightly incised as a rule. In older fish the anal fin sometimes shows a pointed elongation. There is some local varia-tion in the color of the fish. Characteristic, however, is a blue-gray to brownish dorsal coloration, with a paler shade and a silvery lus-ter on the flanks. In fry and juvenile specimens the throat, abdomen, and pectoral, ventral, and anal fins are bright vermilion. This color-ation fades with increasing age, however. The anal and caudal fins have a black margin; the rest of the caudal fin is light in color. The species is generally regarded as being very aggressive. It is possible that the remaining piranhas described here are synonyms, color va-rieties, local races, or subspecies of *Serrasalmus nattereri.* Numer-ous investigations carried out by the author indicate otherwise, however. For this reason it is suggested here for the first time that *Serrasalmus nigricans* be classified as a species in its own right. Where *Serrasalmus notatus* is concerned, the reader is referred to the South American literature already available.

Serrasalmus nigricans
Distribution: Amazon and Orinoco region.

25-28 teeth on the ventral keel. Maximum length about 20-25 cm (8-10 inches). The body is similar in shape to that of *S. nattereri,* but the head and jaws are daintier in build. Juvenile coloration is silvery with numerous black spots. In both young and old specimens, the anal and caudal fins have a black margin, the remainder of the cau-

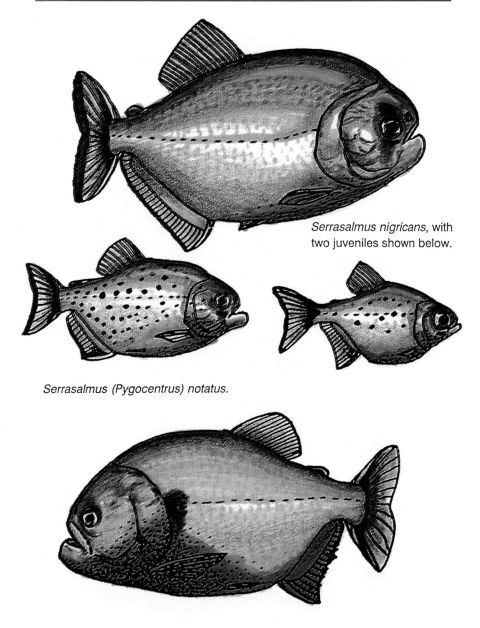

Serrasalmus nigricans, with two juveniles shown below.

Serrasalmus (Pygocentrus) notatus.

dal fin being contrastingly light in color. In most specimens the caudal fin is hardly notched at all. The body color of adult specimens is
predominantly bluish to brownish gray. Unlike *S. nattereri,* neither
immature nor adult fish show any red on the lower regions of the
body or on the fins.

Serrasalmus notatus

Distribution: Orinoco, Lago del Guarico, as well as numerous smaller stagnant and flowing waters in Venezuela.

25-29 teeth on the ventral keel. Body stocky and laterally compressed. Powerfully arched frontal/dorsal region. The body color in both immature and adult fish is predominantly silver with a conspicuous black spot on the flanks that fades slightly in old specimens. All the fins are of a light, translucent coloration, and there is no black caudal margin. The tail fin often shows a dark zone below the caudal peduncle and may possess an asymmetrically elongated lower lobe. Whether immature fish are spotted is not known for certain. Throat, opercula, pectoral and ventral fins, parts of the abdomen, and the anterior portion of the anal fin are bright blood-red in color. In old fish this color may grow very much darker or may fade. Jaws and dentition are conspicuously large and powerful. This extremely aggressive species is called *caribe colorado* and *capaburro* (colored karibe or "the donkey-skinned one," meaning thickskinned) in Venezuela and is feared above all toward the end of the drought.

The research on piranhas has only just begun!

Serrasalmus (Pygocentrus) notatus. Photo by Leo G. Nico.

Serrasalmus (Pygocentrus) notatus

Colossoma bidens, a mimic of *Serrasalmus notatus* above.

The black piranha, *Serrasalmus niger*(?), and its mimic, *Colossoma oculus*.
Upper photo by Leo G. Nico, lower photo by Andre Roth.

Fishing

*...Extracts from the journal kept on my travels
in Venezuela...*

20 March 1980: From Cuidad Bolivar
to Caicara del Orinoco
Fishing in the gigantic stream

After an eight-hour bus journey with Orituco Transport, we reach Caicara del Orinoco at about 1700 hours. The town is not particularly big. White, low houses with dusty roads, mango trees with ripe fruit. The deputy bus driver takes us down to the stream. It is hot, but we are feeling exuberant.

Slowly the massive, loam-gray stream crawls along the sandy bays of its banks. What particularly imprints itself on the mind, however, are the round granite boulders that protrude from the water everywhere and are arranged along the banks of the Orinoco like shields. We choose one of these flat shields of rock as a camping place.

While the other two are busy with sleeping bag, stove, or camera, I reach for rod and line. But first the small box with the tackle has to be unearthed from the lowermost region of the large rucksack. Then I quickly go down to the stream and end up jumping from one boulder to the next until I reach the outermost one. We are a very long way from deep-freezers and supermarkets with overfilled shelves. Let us hope there are fish to be found here; a protein ration would do no harm. Here fishing is an important means of procuring food, and that it happens to be free is an added bonus. But this "pleasant compulsion" is not needed when I look at the mighty tropical river Orinoco.

Another two leaps and I have reached a boulder on the bank. As a lure, I have fixed to the line a metal spinner that mimics an injured, fleeing small fish. The bait has hardly been cast when the first bite is registered! Shortly afterward the first piranha lies inside the pot. Its abdomen is bright red. Many more follow.

They also swallow a bait consisting of piranha flesh and even put their jaws around the empty hook when the line is brought in. They bite through even the thickest of steel leaders. The other members

Blackwater Rio Yabo, Venezuela.

Muddy water in Estado Barinas, Venezuela.

A piranha expedition's camp. Photos by Leo G. Nico.

of the expedition have not remained idle either. While Derk enthusiastically helps with the fishing and, with medical and zoological thoroughness, examines some of the catch, Norbert makes sure that everything is well on the culinary front. From where we are we can hear him busying himself with the rattling saucepans and the stove. We suddenly hear him shout, "All the spices have vanished!" Unperturbed we go on fishing—even amid the greatest chaos inside a rucksack, everything turns up again sooner or later.

The evening atmosphere of the tropical landscape is magnificent. As the sun goes down the most brilliant of colors appear in the sky and in the water of the Orinoco. In a wedge-shaped pattern, hundreds of cormorants move—just above our heads—toward their roosts. The air is full of the swishing of their beating wings. In the shallow water of the neighboring bay, the river dolphins snort. A natural painting, impressive and grand.

All of a sudden, at around 1900 hours, complete darkness falls. The warm tropical night has begun. The rocks are still hot from the sun. Impressed, the three of us sit around the small stove. Dinner consists of watermelon, rice, catfish, and fried piranhas—food for gourmets. The piranhas have an excellent, firm flesh.

25 March 1980: From San Fernando de Apure to Apurito
Dangling above the Rio Apure

After the days on Indian territory, we are traveling by bus through Llanos in the direction of the Andes. The road is accompanied by lagunas (shallow lakes). Everywhere are flocks of white and gray herons, storks, pink spoonbills, and black and red ibises (corocoros). Near some of the watering places lie dead cattle. We also discover our first caimans. Piranhas, too, have been put into the lagoons for "cleansing purposes." Norbert is worn out, sleeps through everything.

We reach the town of San Fernando de Apure, once visited by Humboldt as well. It looks somehow dirty and run down. Already at about 1700 hours, on an overloaded and very shaky old bus, we continue on our journey up the Apure. The sheet-metal covering the floor of the bus is so brittle that a *campesino* (peasant) who is sitting on it is able to throw through the rust holes and cracks straight onto the road, the chicken bones he has picked clean.

By the time we arrive at the small town of Apurito it has already grown dark. A large number of village youngsters follow us about

Clearwater stream in Estado Guarico, Venezuela.

Flooded grasslands in Venezuela. Photos by Leo G. Nico and Donald C. Taphorn.

at first, in amazement. We leave the town as fast as we can. Weighed down by our rucksacks we stumble along the Apure and eventually find a place for our hammocks in a large tree. Thus we fall asleep, at a lofty height, half dangling above the loam-yellow Rio Apure and its piranhas.

In the morning we catch about 25 big piranhas. I dissect the jaws of the biggest animals. We gut six of the fish and bake them in a pot. Breakfast consists of "piranhaburgers" inside bread rolls with tomato ketchup. They smell delicious.

28 March 1980: From Mantecal to Bruzual
Fishing for piranhas in a lagoon

The bus continues to rattle along toward Bruzual, the last town on the upper Rio Apure. The road surface varies between metal and asphalt full of holes. Sleeping is impossible; the rucksacks keep jumping about and need to be wedged in again with unfailing regularity. We arrive toward the evening, by which time we are sweaty and dusty. I run down to the Rio Apure with rod and line. The water is low and there is a very strong current. No fish get caught.

Back to the first muddy lagoon, a one-time tributary of the Apure that I had passed earlier. Now the fish are practically leaping about here. It is 1815 hours. The sun is already very low by the time I cast the spinner. No sooner has it splashed onto the surface than the line starts whizzing off the reel. I stop the first, explosive escape with a strong stroke. Irritated, the *caribe* darts left and right, zig-zagging. But all the time I manage to pull the fish closer and closer to the bank. When I finally pull the fish ashore I have to take care not to disappear in the mud. About 30 meters away, the heads of two *babas* (caimans) stick out of the water. Their eyes follow my every move as I release the hook. There is an endless supply of mosquitos, too. Within the shortest possible time the troublesome bloodsuckers subject me to over 40 bites on my arms, hands, and face.

I cast a few more times, and suddenly the rod almost gets pulled out of my hand. It is already getting dark by the time I land a stocky and powerful piranha with a length of about 25 cm (10 inches). This fish is noticeably darker in coloration than the other piranhas of the same length I have caught. The caudal and dorsal fins, too, are almost completely black. Whether this is a real black piranha or another subspecies may remain a mystery until I get home and a proper examination becomes possible. Although the rucksack is heavy enough as it is, a last plastic bag with formalin is added to its contents. The bag weighs about 1 kilogram (2.2 pounds) and contains the most impressive fish in the world.

Fishing Tackle

Rod: Suitable above all are strong telescopic rods made of hollow glass with a length of 2.5 to 3.5 meters (8¼-11½ feet) and a casting weight of 40 to 80 grams (1½-3 oz.) for good distances.

Reel: A solid stationary reel or possibly a high-speed reel.

The Takuna Indians make masks with piranha's teeth. They also made this balsa wood shark. Do thresher sharks ever get thousands of miles from the ocean to where these Indians live? Photo by Dr. Herbert R. Axelrod.

Line: A thickness of 0.35 mm-0.40 mm is recommended.

Steel leader and spinner: A steel leader is absolutely essential. Only extremely strong steel leaders (0.40 mm and upward) and strong barrel spinners with swivel-hooks should be used!

Artificial baits: Generally speaking, all light-colored, silvery or golden artificial baits made of metal are suitable (they are intended for use on dark days but in this case are needed because of the cloudy water conditions). The color combination red/white also proved highly effective. Spoons and spinners up to 25 grams (1 oz.). Where there are overhanging or sunken trees, weedless spoons are more successful. If necessary, the treble hook can be replaced with a single hook size 2/0. Not infrequently the treble hooks had their shanks bitten off, since the jaws of piranhas operate as effectively as metal shears. As compared with ordinary spoons baits, spinners with a rotating spoon proved markedly more successful. Baits made of plastic and rubber are useless, as they get chewed to bits instantly!

Natural baits: On long-shanked hooks (size 1/0-4/0), with a steel leader in front:
- bits of flesh cut off dead piranhas;
- a whole young piranha, sacrificed;
- fresh, bleeding ox heart, liver, etc.

A float usually is not required. The bait is simply allowed to sink and is often taken while this is happening. Where the casting involves greater distances, a float can be useful, although not infrequently it gets chewed.

Important Hints

Useful small items that form an absolutely essential part of the fishing equipment include:
- a sharp knife;
- jaw-lever and hook release;
- mosquito repellent (liquid, spray, vitamin-B tablets, etc.). My own experience has taught me, however, that even the most praised mosquito repellents do not always prevent that multitude of red welts! A pair of full-length trousers and a wind-proof jacket with long sleeves often suffice to prevent the worst;
- headgear (to prevent sunstroke);
- sunglasses (preferably polarized).

Before the hook is released, every freshly caught piranha should be thoroughly stunned with strong blows on the head and afterward

A *Serrasalmus (Pristobrycon)* species from the Orinoco basin.

Serrasalmus elongatus, still hooked.

Serrasalmus altuvei, a preserved specimen. Photos by Leo G. Nico.

Serrasalmus eigenmanni.

Serrasalmus (Pygocentrus) striolatus. Photos by Leo G. Nico.

killed with the knife inserted into the head or heart. Releasing the hook when the animal is still alive, wildly thrashing, and, above all, snapping about is fraught with considerable danger.

The jaws are armed with razor-sharp triangular teeth, and the extremely strong jaw musculature facilities snap at lightning speed. This enables the piranhas not only to chop off careless fingers and toes but also—and above all—to cause deep flesh wounds to the angler that bleed copiously. Another very important fact to note is that due to continuing nerve impulses, even freshly killed animals can still snap dangerously.

Traveling in tropical regions invariably entails some health risks, and these should be reduced through vaccination. In addition to taking tablets to prevent malaria (which is essential in any case), anyone traveling to South America is urged to have the following vaccinations before embarking on the journey:

- vaccination against yellow fever (by injection);
- vaccination against hepatitis (an injection to prevent inflammations of the liver);
- typhoid and paratyphoid vaccinations;
- where necessary, booster vaccinations against smallpox and tetanus. A smallpox vaccination is not a condition for entering Venezuela unless the traveler is arriving from Ethiopia, Kenya, or Somalia. A vaccination against cholera only becomes compulsory for journeys from or through countries where this infectious disease is rife.

A valid passport is accepted as an identity card throughout South America. Applications for a visa must be made to the relevent embassies.

Seining for piranhas at Cano Maporal, Estado Apure, Venezuela. Photo by Leo G. Nico.

At a small tributary of the Rio Marmelos flowing into the Rio Madeira, Dr. Axelrod caught this *Serrasalmus (Pristobrycon)* species. It might well be a juvenile *Serrasalmus striolatus.* The black spots on the fish are encysted larvae of worms (parasites) that are carried by birds. Fishes with these black parasites are usually found around trees in which fish-eating birds are perched. Photo by Dr. Herbert R. Axelrod.

Summary

Piranhas occur mainly in the whitewater rivers of South America. They were discovered by European conquistadores around 1533. Long before that, the piranhas were already known to the South American Indians in these regions and in one form or another occupied a place in some of the Indian cultures.

The body of these fish is stocky and compressed, which indicates that their main habitat consists of slow-flowing and stagnant waters. Piranhas possess an impressively sharp and strong dentition. Their feeding behavior makes them unique among freshwater fishes and is identical only to that of the sharks (morsels of food are torn off and even large prey is attacked without fear).

The dangerousness of piranhas in relation to man is often exaggerated. In Venezuela, at least, its degree varies and is clearly and closely linked to the annual cycle of the tropical climate. During the drought, the habitats shrink due to evaporation and the resultant great shortage of food leads to increased aggressiveness of the fish. In the rainy season, small rivers are transformed into vast floodplains. Now the natives bathe in the waters they so anxiously avoided before. It seems very likely that factors such as brood-care instinct during the spawning season, water pollution with bloody refuse, and the splashing and struggling of wounded creatures increase the risk of an attack by piranhas, but it is impossible to draw up any hard and fast rules. It can happen, for example, that certain stretches of a river are regarded as risky while a few kilometers upstream or down-stream no attacks ever occur. Healthy and uninjured animals and humans are seldom attacked!

By devouring sick, weak, and dead animals, piranhas in the tropical waters of South America undertake an exceedingly important ecological function. Without them, disastrous epidemics might re-

Serrasalmus (Pygocentrus) piraya. Photo by Dr. Herbert R. Axelrod.

An unidentified piranha, probably photographed in a public aquarium. Note the teeth projecting above the gum line. Photo by Hansen.

sult, particularly after catastrophic floods. Piranhas appear to be largely resistant to fungal diseases, which also points toward their function as scavengers. Severe oxygen shortages are clearly tolerated better by piranhas—with the aid of frequent trips to the surface for air—than by many other fishes.

Keeping piranhas presents no problems. In tanks that are too small, however, piranhas invariably show a "jumpy," nervous reaction. Members of the same species that are weak, sick, or injured bring out the cannibalism in them. Smaller injuries caused by biting, on the other hand, regenerate surprisingly quickly.

Breeding piranhas in captivity can be achieved by raising the water temperature in the tank to about 30°C (86°F). External sex differences are not visible. Piranhas are the only characins which practice genuine brood care. They guard their nest and in the early stages defend their fast-growing brood (in the author's tanks, piranha fry 3.5 cm [1½ inches] long grew to nearly 10 cm [4 inches] in four months).

Scientific knowledge and the classification of the various species are largely in their infancy where piranhas are concerned.

Catching piranhas is very easy. Because of their protein content, the fact that they are common, and not least the pleasant taste of their flesh, they are even of some economic importance in parts of South America.

A close-up of the face of a red-bellied piranha, *Serrasalmus nattereri*. No one knows what the nasal flaps do.

Index

An undescribed piranha from Brazil. Tentatively it is known as *Serrasalmus (Pristobrycon)* "Iridescent." Photo by Leo G. Nico and Donald C. Taphorn.